Native American Directory

Vital Records of Maine, Massachusetts, Rhode Island, Connecticut, New York and Wisconsin

Researched and compiled by
Lorraine (Rainwaters) Henry
in partnership with the
guiding spirit of
Aquina A Co Eechee
(Jane Curtis Joseph Waters)

Formatted by:
Jeanine Osborne Liggins
Under the spiritual guidance
of
Wanita Lindsey Osborne

HERITAGE BOOKS
2006

HERITAGE BOOKS

AN IMPRINT OF HERITAGE BOOKS, INC.

Books, CDs, and more—Worldwide

For our listing of thousands of titles see our website
at
www.HeritageBooks.com

Published 2006 by
HERITAGE BOOKS, INC.
Publishing Division
65 East Main Street
Westminster, Maryland 21157-5026

International Standard Book Number: 978-0-7884-0896-8

Dedicated to:

Mandred

Tyler

Jazz

Amber

And all those of the seventh generation

b = born

d = died

s = son

d = daughter

ca = circa   (used to figure approximate date, etc.)

BIRTHS

BIRTHS

AARON, JOSEPH - b. May 12, 1738, s. Sarah
Muckamug (Indian) & Joseph, Cumberland, R.I.

ABEL - b. s. Saucoauso (Jeptha); grandson
of Chief Sachem of Nantucket, Wanack-Mamak

ABEL, BEN - b. s. Abel; grandson of Saucoauso (Jeptha);
great grandson of Wanack-Mamack, Chief Sachem
of Nantucket Islands, Ma.

ABEL, CAIN - b. s. Abel; grandson of Saucoauso
(Jeptha); great grandson of Wanack-Mamack, Chief
Sachem of Nantucket Islands, Ma.

ABIMILECK - b. s. Attawanhood & Sougonusk;
grandson of Uncas; great-grandson of Pequot Sachem,
Sassacus of Ct. lands

ABIMELECK, ESTHER - b. 1695, Ct., d. Abimeleck

ABRAHAM, ANDREW JR. - b. Grafton, Ma.

ADAMS, EMELINE - b. Brothertown, NY, d. Samuel
& Mary (Fowler) Adams

ADAMS, HANNAH - b. Brothertown, NY, d. Samuel
& Mary (Fowler) Adams

ADAMS, JOHN - b. 1755, Brothertown, NY, s. John
& Sarah Adams

ADAMS, PHILENA - b. Farmington, Ct., d. Solomon
& Olive

ADAMS, SAMUEL - b. 1734, s. Quinnipiac Indian of
East Haven, Ct.

ADAMS, SARAH - b. d. John and Sarah Adams of
Tunxis Tribe; Farmington, Ct.

ADAMS, SOLOMON - b. s. Samuel and Hannah
Squamp of Wangunk Tribe; Middletown, Ct.; res.
Lot 52, Farmington, Ct.

ADAMS, THANKFUL - b. d. Samuel & Mary Fowler,
Brothertown, NY

AHANO - b. s. Sequassen, Sachem of Tunxis Tribe;
Farmington, Ct.

AHAWAYETSQUAINE (JOAN) - b. Natick, Ma. d. of
Poquanum

ALVIS, BETHIA - b. ca. 1856, d. Charles F. and
Jemima Alvis, Mashpee Tribe; Mashpee, Ma.

1

BIRTHS

ALVIS, CLARISSA - b. ca. 1847, d. Sampson E. &
Hannah G. Alvis, Mashpee Tribe; Mashpee, Ma.

ALVIS, EZEKIEL - b. ca. 1836, s. Sampson E. & Hannah
G. Alvis, Mashpee Tribe; Mashpee, Ma.

ALVIS, MARYANN - b. ca. 1854, d. Charles F. and
Jemima Alvis, Mashpee Tribe; Mashpee, Ma.

AMAPOO - b. Sanchecantacket (Edgartown) d. Cheesechamut,
(Nickanoose) Sachem of Holmes Hole, Martha's Vineyard

AMAPOO, SARAH - b. ca. 1865, R.I., d. Charles
Anthony

AMMONS, ALEXANDER R. - b. ca. 1848, Charlestown,
R.I.; s. Gideon L. Ammons; res., Providence, R.I.

AMMONS, CLARENCE G. - b. ca. 1873, s. Mary E.
& George G. Ammons, Westerly, R.I.

AMMONS, EMMA J. - b. ca. 1858, R.I.; d. Alexander
R. Ammons

AMMONS, GEORGE G. - b. ca. 1856, R.I., res.,
Westerly, R.I.

AMMONS, HATTIE - b. ca. 1876, R.I. d. Alexander
R. Ammons

AMMONS, JOSEPH - b. ca. 1808, Charlestown, R.I.

AMMONS, JUDITH - b. ca. 1808, Charlestown, R.I.

AMOS, ABIAH - b., Martha's Vineyard, d. of Jonathan &
Rachel Amos

AMOS, AURELIUS E. - b. ca. 1853, s. Matthias &
Clarissa Amos, Mashpee Tribe

AMOS, BENJAMIN F. - b. ca. 1850, d. Joseph &
Phebe R. Amos, Mashpee Tribe; Mashpee, Ma.

AMOS, CELINA H. - b. ca. 1860, d. Matthias &
Clarissa Amos, Mashpee Tribe; Mashpee, Ma.

AMOS, CLARINDA C. - b. ca. 1846, d. Matthias &
Clarissa Amos, Mashpee Tribe; Mashpee, Ma.

AMOS, CORDELIA B. - b. ca. 1847, d. Joseph &
Phebe Amos, Mashpee Tribe; Mashpee, Ma.

AMOS, ELIZABETH - b. ca. 1856, d. Delia Amos,
Mashpee Tribe, Mashpee, Ma.

AMOS, FRANKLIN H. - b. ca. 1860, s. Daniel Q.
Amos, Mashpee Tribe; res., Mashpee, Ma.

BIRTHS

AMOS, HORATIO M. - b. ca. 1856, s. Matthias &
Clarissa Amos, Mashpee Tribe; Mashpee, Ma.

AMOS, LUCINDA - b. ca. 1858, d. Delia Amos, Mashpee
Tribe; res., Mashpee, Ma,

AMOS, MARY - b., Martha's Vineyard, d. Jonathan &
Rachel Amos

AMOS, REBECCA C. - b. ca. 1837, d. Joseph & Phebe
R. Amos, Mashpee Tribe; res., Mashpee, Ma.

AMOS, SARAH B. - b. ca. 1845, d. Joseph & Phebe R. Amos,
Mashpee Tribe; res., Mashpee, Ma.

ANDERSON, EDWARD - b. ca. 1820, Hopkinton, R.I.
s. Candis Babcock

ANTHONY, CHARLES - b. ca. 1830, Worcester County,
Ma. s. Charlotte (Daniels) Anthony; res., Boston, Ma.

ANTHONY, CHARLES B. - b. ca. 1865, R.I. s. Charles
Anthony

ANTHONY, JOHN D. - b. ca. 1811, Charlestown, R.I.
res., Palmer, Ma.

ANTHONY, JOHN - b. ca. 1815, Ma.

ANTHONY, JOSEPH - b., Dec. 24, 1753, Grafton, Ma.,
s. of Joseph & Abigail Printer Anthony

ANTHONY, JOSEPH S. - b. 1848, Aug 8, Christiantown, Ma.

ANTHONY, RACHEL - b. 1844, Aug 9, Christiantown, Ma.,
d. John Anthony and Betsey Mingo; res., Gay Head, Ma.

ANTHONY, SAMUEL JOHNSON - b. ca. 1860, s. Sarah
Johnson

ANTHONY, SARAH - b. ca. 1865, R.I. d. Charles Anthony

APES, EMELINE W. - b. ca. 1851, Ashford, Ct., d. Mary
Ann Jones; res., Middletown, Ct.

ASKOMOPOO - b. d. Isaac Nickanoose (Cheeschaamog)

ASSWETOUGH - b. d. John Sassamon

ATTAQUIN, LEWIS ELLIS -b. ca. 1846, s. Solomon & Cynthia
Attaquin, Mashpee/Herring Pond Tribe; res., Mashpee, Ma.

ATTAQUIN, PAMELA - b. ca. 1850, d. Benjamin J.
Attaquin, Mashpee Tribe; Mashpee, Ma.

ATTAQUIN, PERSIS A. - b. ca. 1853, s. Benjamin J. Attaquin,
Mashpee Tribe; Mashpee, Ma.

ATTAWANHOOD - b. s. Uncas; grandson of Great
Pequot Sachem, Sassacus of Ct. lands

3

BIRTHS

ATTOMON, CHRISTIAN - b. s. Richard Attoman;
grandson Attamonchassuck of Potonumecot Tribe,
Chaquesett (Harwich, Ma.) area

ATTOMON, ESTHER - b. d. Richard Attoman;
grandson Attamonchassuck of Potonumecot Tribe
Chaquesett (Harwich, Ma.) area

ATTOMON, EXPERIENCE - b. d. Richard & Hester
Attoman; Chaquesett Neck, Ma.; granddaughter of
Attamonchassuck of Potonumecot Tribe;

ATTOMON, HOSEA - b. d. Richard & Hester
Attoman; Chaquesett Neck, Ma.; granddaughter of
Attamonchassuck of Potonumecot Tribe;

ATTOMON, LYDIA - b. d. Richard Attoman;
Granddaughter of Attamonchassuck of Potonumec Tribe;
Harwich, Ma. area

ATTOMON, REBECCA - b. d. Attamonchassuck of
Potonumecot Tribe; res. Chaquesett, Harwich, Ma.

ATTOMON, RICHARD - b. d. Attamonchassuck of
Potonumecot Tribe; Harwich, Ma.

ATTOMON, RICHARD - b. s. Richard & Hester
Attomon; Chaquesett Neck, Ma.; grandson of
Attamonchassuck of Potonumecot Tribe; res.
Harwich Ma.

ATTOMONCHASSUCK, JOHN - b. s. Attamonchassuck
& wife Betty of Potonumecot Tribe; res., Chaquesett
(Harwich, Ma.) area

ATTOMONCHASSUCK, JOSEPH - b. s. Attamonchassuck
& wife Betty of Potonumecot Tribe; res., Chaquesett
(Harwich, Ma.) area

ATTOMONCHASSUCK, SARAH - b. d. Attamonchassuck
and wife Betty of Potonumecot Tribe; res., Chaquesett
(Harwich, Ma.) area

AWASSAMOG, AMOS - b. s. John Awassamog and
Yawatta; grandson of Nanempashamet; Natick Indian

AWASSAMOG, JOHN - b. ca. 1614; a Nipnet Indian;
nephew to Chief Wuttawushan res., at Winnisimet (Chelsea)

AWASSAMOG, JOSHUA - b. s. John Awassamog and
Yawatta; grandson of Nanempashamet; Natick Indian

BIRTHS

AWASSAMOG, SAMUEL - b. s .John Awassamog and Yawatta; grandson of Nanempashamet; Natick Indian

AWASSAMOG, THOMAS - b. s. John Awassamog and Yawattta; grandson of Nanempashamet; res., Framingham, Ma.

BABCOCK, ANNA - b. ca. 1843, Charlestown, R.I.; res., Hopkinton, R.I.

BABCOCK, ANNA - b. ca. 1872, d. Anna Babcock, Hopkinton, R.I.

BABCOCK, CHARLES - b. ca.1868, d. Anna Babcock, Hopkinton, R.I.

BABCOCK, CORA BELL - b. ca.1878, d. Anna Babcock, Hopkinton, R.I.

BABCOCK, D.A. - b. ca. 1862, d. Anna Babcock, Hopkinton, R.I.

BABCOCK, EMMA - b. ca. 1866, d. Anna Babcock, Hopkinton, R.I.

BABCOCK, FRANCIS - b.ca. 1880, d. Anna Babcock, Hopkinton, R.I.

BABCOCK, MINNIE - b. ca. 1875, d. Anna Babcock, Hopkinton, R.I.

BAKER, LOUISA E. - b. ca. 1845, d. Samuel and Sophronia Baker; Yarmouth Tribe; Yarmouth, Ma.

BAKER, MARTHA E. - b. ca.1849, d. Samuel and Sophronia Baker; Yarmouth Tribe; Yarmouth, Ma.

BAKER, SUSAN H. - b. ca. 1850, d. Samuel and Sophronia Baker; Yarmouth Tribe, Yarmouth, Ma.

BAKER, THATCHER - b. ca. 1843, s. Samuel and Sophronia Baker; Yarmouth Tribe, Yarmouth, Ma.

BAKER, WM. HENRY - b. ca. 1843, s. Samuel and Sophronia Baker; Yarmouth Tribe; res., Yarmouth, Ma.

BAKERMAN, CHARLES R. - b. ca. 1859, d. Josiah and Helen Bakerman, Dudley Tribe; res., Northampton, Ma.

BANCROFT, LYDIA ANN - b. ca. 1857, d. Jeremiah Bancroft, Punkapog Tribe; res., Canton, Ma.

BANCROFT, MARY ELIZABETH - b. ca. 1860, d. Jeremiah Bancroft, Punkapog Tribe; res., Canton, Ma.

BASSETT, BETHIAH J. - b. 1849, July, Gay Head, Ma., d. Leander and Huldah Jeffers, res., Gay Head, Ma.

BIRTHS

BASSET, JULIA - b. 1841, June 11, d. Leander &
Huldah Basset

BASSET, LEANDER - b. 1810., Oct. 15, Farmeck,
Edgartown, Ma., d. James and Esther (Sharper) Bassett;
res., Gay Head, Ma.,

BEARSE, JOSEPH - b. 1652, s. Mary (Hyano) and
Austin (Augustine) Bearse; descendant of Sachem
Iyanough, Hyanis, Ma.

BEARSE, JOSIAH - b. 1718, s. Joseph Bearse and
Martha (Taylor) of Yarmouth, Ma; descendant of
Iyanough, Hyanis, Ma.

BELAIN, ALONZO - b. 1850, Dec.6, Gay Head, Ma.,
s. George J. and Sophia (Peters); res., Gay Head, Ma.

BELAIN, DANIEL W. - b. 1854, Aug.11, Gay Head,
Ma., s. George J. and Sophia (Peters); res., Gay Head, Ma.

BELAIN, GEORGE J. - b. 1813, Nov., Chappaquiddick,
Ma., s. Peter and Sarah (Johnson) Belain; res.,
Chappaquiddick, Ma.

BELAIN, JOHN W. - b. 1859, Aug. 26, Gay Head, Ma.,
s. George J. and Sophia Peters; res., Gay Head, Ma.

BELAIN, LUCRETIA - b. ca. 1834, d. Isaiah and Lawra
Belain, Chappaquiddick Tribe; res., Chappaquiddick , Ma.

BELAIN, MARY B. - b. ca. 1850, d. David and Harriet R.
Belain, Chappequiddick Tribe; Chappaquiddick, Ma.

BELAIN, MATILDA S. - b. ca. 1855, d. David and Harriet
R. Belain, Chappaquiddick Tribe; Chappaquiddick, Ma.

BELAIN, MELISSA - b. 1837, Apr. 10, d. George J.
& Sophia (Peters) Belain

BENT, BETSEY - b. ca. 1841, Charlestown, R.I.; res.,
Bristol, R.I.

BENT, WILLIAM H. - b. ca. 1847, Charlestown, R.I.; res.,
Providence, R.I.

BERETAN, HARRY (Poitan, Harry) - b. s. Masauquet;
grandson of Attapehat (Autopcat, Autopscot)

BLODGET, EBEN A. - b. ca. 1851, s. Amos A. and
Patience Blodget, Natick Tribe; res. Natick, Ma.

BLODGET, FLORENCE I. - b. ca. 1859, d. Amos A.
and Patience Blodget, Natick Tribe; res., Natick, Ma.

BIRTHS

BLODGET, MARY H. - b. ca. 1854, d. Amos A. and
Patience Blodget, Natick Tribe; res., Natick, Ma.

BOYDEN, CHARLES Wm. - b. ca. 1840, s. Deborah
Boyden, Dartmouth Tribe; res., Dartmouth, Ma.

BOYDEN, JOSEPH - b. ca. 1845, s. Deborah Boyden,
Dartmouth Tribe; res., Dartmouth, Ma.

BOYDEN, NATHANIEL A. - b. ca. 1839, s. Deborah
Boyden, Dartmouth Tribe; res., Dartmouth, Ma.

BROOKS, JOHN - b. ca. 1836, s. Nancy Brooks of
Yarmouth Tribe; Yarmouth, Ma.

BROOKS, MARY A. - b. ca. 1839, d. Nancy Brooks of
Yarmouth Tribe; Yarmouth, MA.

BROOKS, SYLVESTER - b. ca. 1841, s. Nancy Brooks
of Yarmouth Tribe; Yarmouth, Ma.

BROWN, ANDREW J. - b. ca. 1855, Boston, Ma.; res.,
Worcester, Ma.

BROWN, ANNIE F. - b. ca. 1852, Boston, Ma.; res.
Worcester, Ma.

BROWN, AZARIAH G. - b. ca. 1848, s. John D. and
Sarah Brown, Mashpee Tribe; res., Mashpee, Ma.

BROWN, C. LEWIS - b. ca. 1858, Richmond, R.I.; res.,
Carolina Mills

BROWN, CHARLES W. - b. ca. 1844, s. William &
Mary J. Brown, Hassanamisco Tribe; res., Framingham, Ma.

BROWN, EDWIN - b. ca. 1851, s. William and Mary J.
Brown, Hassanamisco Tribe; res., Framingham, Ma.

BROWN, EMELINE - b. 1850, d. John D. and Sarah
Brown, Mashpee Tribe; res., Mashpee, Ma.

BROWN, ESTHER R. - b. ca. 1853, South Kingstown,
d. John Noka

BROWN, ESTHER - b. ca. 1858, Richmond, R.I.

BROWN, FREDERICK V. - b. ca.1875, R.I . s. Sarah A.
and Henry H. Brown

BROWN, HANNAH - b. ca. 1811, Charlestown, R.I.

BROWN, HENRY H. - b. ca.1 851; res., South Kingstown,
R.I.

BROWN, HOWARD - b. ca. 1869, s. Sarah E. Brown of
Providence, R.I.

BIRTHS

BROWN, ISABELLA E. - b. ca. 1861, Westerly, R.I., res., Providence, R.I.

BROWN, JOHN E. - b. ca. 1847, Providence, R.I.; res., Providence, R.I.

BROWN, LEWIS C. - b. ca. 1858, Richmond, R.I.; res., Carolina Mills

BROWN, MARTIE P. - b. ca. 1854, Charlestown, R.I.; res., Richmond, R.I.

BROWN, MARY E. - b. ca. 1856, d. William and Mary J. Brown, Hassanisco Tribe; res., Framingham, Ma.

BROWN, MARY E. - b. ca.1860, d. William and Mercy H. Brown, Mashpee Tribe; Mashpee, Ma.

BROWN, SARAH A. - b. ca.1851, d. John D. and Sarah Brown, Mashpee Tribe; res., Mashpee, Ma.

BROWN, SARAH E. - b. ca. 1842, Providence, R.I.

BROWN, SOPHRONIA - b. ca.1857, Richmond, R.I.; res., Narragansett Pier

BROWN, THADDEUS - b. ca. 1873, R.I., s. Sarah A. and Henry H. Brown

BROWN, THEODORE D. - b. ca. 1877, s. Sarah A. and Henry H. Brown

BRUSHELL, HENRY - b. 1814, June 24, s. Abigail (Skeesuck) and Samuel Brushel, res., Brothertown, NY

BRUSHELL, LORINDA - b. d. Betsey (Ceipet) and Sampson Brushel; res., lots 127, 34 at Brothertown, NY

BRUSHELL, MARY E. - b.ca. 1831, Stonington, Ct.

BRUSHELL, SAMPSON - b. 1774, s. Abigail Brushel of Brotherton, NY, lot 25

BRUSHELL, SAMUEL - b. 1712, s. Abigail Brushel of Brothertown, NY, lot 25

BUCHANAN, MARY - b. daughter of Thomas & Patience (Durfee) Buchanan

BUNKER, TAMSON - b. 1805, July 12, Gay Head, Ma., d. Betsey Bunker

BURNE, SARAH - b. 1744, Nov. 27, Grafton, Ma, d. of Forten & Sarah (Aaron) Burne

BURNE, FORTIN - b. s. of Fortin Burne

BURR, ALONZO - b. ca. 1844, s. Eli and Saloma Burr, Oneida Tribe

8

BIRTHS

BURR, ALBERT - b. ca. 1851, s. Eli and Saloma Burr,
Oneida Tribe

BURR, ANN E. - b. ca. 1847, d. Lemuel and Mary Burr,
Punkapog Tribe; res., Cambridgeport, Ma.

BURR, FIDELIA - b. ca. 1842, d. Eli and Saloma Burr,
Oneida Tribe; res., Springfield, Ma.

BURR, LEMUEL - b. ca. 1849, s. Lemuel and Mary Burr,
Punkapog Tribe; res., Cambridgeport, Ma.

BURR, MARY - b. ca. 1855, d. Lemuel and Mary Burr,
Punkapog Tribe; res., Cambridgeport, Ma.

BURR, SALLY L. - b. ca. 1857, d. Lemuel and Mary Burr,
Punkapog Tribe; res., Cambridgeport, Ma.

BURR, SAMANTHA - b. ca. 1845, d. Eli and Saloma Burr,
Oneida Tribe

BURR, VIANNA - b. ca. 1840, d. Eli and Saloma Burr,
Oneida Tribe; res., Springfield, Ma.

BURRILL, BEAUTY J. - b. ca. 1858, d. David L. and
Olive A. Burrill, Punkapog Tribe; Canton, Ma.

BURRILL, OLIVE ELLA - b. ca. 1852, d. David L.
and Olive A. Burrill, Punkapog Tribe; Canton, Ma.

BUTLER, IDA - b. ca. d. William H. and Sarah H. Butler,
Mashpee Tribe; Mashpee, Ma.

CAHKUHQUIT, SARAH - b. d. Samson & Elizabeth
Cahkuhquit

CAIN, JEMIMA - b. d. Cain

CARPENTER, ASA - b. ca. 1863, R.I.

CARPENTER, CHARLES - b. ca. 1875, s. Charles O.
Carpenter of Norwich,Ct.

CARPENTER, CHARLES O. - b. ca. 1848, Stonington,
s. Isaac Carpenter; res., Norwich Ct.

CARPENTER, DELFOLO - b. ca. 1859, R.I.

CARPENTER, DORA - b. ca. 1866, R.I.

CARPENTER, ELIZA - b. ca. 1873, R.I.

CARPENTER, ELIZABETH - b. ca. 1863, R.I.

CARPENTER, HARRIET - b. d. Isaac Taylor & a
Narraganset woman who was daughter to Rhuahamer
Malbone of Woodville

CARPENTER, HARRIET - b. ca. 1843; res., Ct.; became
mother of 10 children

BIRTHS

CARPENTER, HARRY GENET-b. ca. 1868, s. Harriet
Carpenter

CARPENTER, HENRY - b. ca. 1873, s. Charles O.
Carpenter of Norwich

CARPENTER, MARY A. - b. ca. 1832, Narraganset
Reservation; res. Providence, R.I.

CARPENTER, MARY (NOKA) - b. ca. 1840, Providence,
R.I., d. Peter Noka; res. Westerly, R.I.

CASH, BARZILLAI - b. ca. 1844, s. Deborah J. Cash,
Yarmouth Tribe; res, Yarmouth, Ma.

CASH, CHARLES EDWARD - b. ca. 1843, s. Deborah
J. Cash, Yarmouth Tribe; res., Yarmouth, Ma.

CASH, ELIZA ANN - b. ca. 1850, d. Deborah J. Cash,
Yarmouth Tribe; res., Yarmouth, Ma.

CASH, GEORGE HENRY - b. ca. 1852, s. Deborah J.
Cash, Yarmouth Tribe; res., Yarmouth, Ma.

CASH, LEANDER - b. ca. 1846, s. Deborah J. Cash,
Yarmouth Tribe; res., Yarmouth, Ma.

CASH, LUCY ELLEN - b. ca. 1848, d. Deborah J. Cash,
Yarmouth Tribe; res., Yarmouth, Ma.

CATAPAZET - b. s. Cushawashet (Harmon Garret,
Wequashook)

CEASAR - b. Mohegan Indian , s. Oweneco; grandson of
Uncas, Montville, Ct.

CEASAR, ANN - b. d. Mohegan Sachem, Ceasar

CEASAR, AURELIA - b. ca. 1853, d. Lucy Ann Ceasar,
Mashpee Tribe; res., Mashpee, Ma.

CEASAR, LUCY ANN - b. ca. 1832, d. Lucy Ann Ceasar,
Mashpee Tribe; res., Mashpee, Ma.

CHAMPLIN, ABRAHAM - b. ca. 1836, Charlestown, R.I.,
s. Sarah Champlin; res., South Kingstown, R.I.

CHAMPLIN, ABRAHAM L - b. ca. 1867, s. Sarah and
Abraham R. Champlin of Kingstown, R.I.

CHAMPLIN, BENJAMIN R. - b. ca. 1842, Charlestown,
R.I.; res., Providence, R.I.

CHAMPLIN, BETSEY - b. ca. 1817, Westerly, R.I.;
res., Westerly, R.I.

CHAMPLIN, CHARLES A. - b. ca. 1869, s. Sarah and
Abraham R. Champlin of Kingstown, R.I.

BIRTHS

CHAMPLIN, ELIZABETH - b. ca. 1810, Kingston, R.I.; res. Westerly, R.I.

CHAMPLIN, ELLEN M. - b. ca. 1863, d. Mary (Helm) and Benjamin R.Champlin

CHAMPLIN, FREDDIE D. - b. ca. 1871, s. Sarah and Abraham R. Champlin

CHAMPLIN, GEORGE A. - b. ca. 1863, Westerly, R.I.;

CHAMPLIN, GEORGE H. - b. ca. 1857, South Kingstown, R.I., s. Henry Champlin

CHAMPLIN, HANNAH F. - b. ca. 1847, Charlestown, R.I., res., Westerly, R.I.

CHAMPLIN, HENRY H. - b. ca. 1865, s. Sarah and Abraham R. Champlin of South Kingstown, R.I.

CHAMPLIN, IDA - b. ca. 1859, Richmond; res. Westerly, R.I.

CHAMPLIN, JAMES H. - b. ca. 1875, s. Sarah and Abraham R. Champlin

CHAMPLIN, JANE R. - b. ca. 1866, d. Mary (Helm) and Benjamin R. Champlin

CHAMPLIN, LYDIA - b. ca. 1841, Charlestown, R.I.

CHAMPLIN, MARY - b. ca. 1840, Providence, R.I.

CHAMPLIN, MARY R. - b. ca. 1851, Griswold, Ct.

CHAMPLIN, PRISCILLA - b. sister to Abraham R. Champlin

CHAMPLIN, SAMUEL R. - b. ca.

CHAMPLIN, SARAH - b. ca. 1804, South Kingstown; res., Charlestown, R.I.

CHAMPLIN, WALTER H. - b. ca. 1871, s. Mary (Helm) and Benjamin R. Champlin

CHAMPLIN, WILLIAM - b. ca. 1845, Charlestown, R.I.; res., Westerly, R.I.

CHARLES, JOB - b. 1789, Brothertown

CHASE, FRANKLIN H. - b. ca. 1844, s. George W. & Nancy J. Chase, Yarmouth Tribe; res., Yarmouth, Ma.

CHASE, GEORGE W. - b. ca. 1852, s. George W. and Nancy J. Chase,Yarmouth Tribe; res.,Yarmouth, Ma.

CHEESCHAAMOG, CALEB - b. s. Cheshechaamog (Isaac Nickanoose)

BIRTHS

CHEEVES, NANCY (NOKA) - b. 1815, South Kingston, d. Sam Noka; spouse to George Cheeves, res., Charlestown, R.I.

CHESHECHAAMOG - b. s. Wauwinet (Pomhaman), the Sachem of Holmes Hole, Martha's Vineyard, Ma.

CISCO, JAMES L. - b. ca. s. Samuel and Sarah Maria Cisco, Hassanamisco Tribe; res., Grafton, Ma.

CISCO, LEWIS S. - b. ca. 1858, s. Samuel and Sarah Maria Cisco, Hassanamisco Tribe; res., Grafton, Ma.

CISCO, SAMUEL - b. ca. 1856, s. Samuel and Sarah Maria Cisco, Hassanamisco Tribe; res., Grafton, Ma.

CISCO, SARAH C. M. - b. ca. 1859, d. Samuel and Sarah Maria Cisco, Hassanamisco Tribe; res., Grafton, Ma.

CISCO, WILLIAM S. - b. ca. 1852, s. Samuel and Sarah Maria Cisco, Hassanamisco Tribe; res., Grafton, Ma.

CLARK, CHARLES - b. ca. 1840, Charlestown, R.I.; res. Richmond

CLARK, JOHN - b. ca. 1866, s. Charles Clark of Richmond

COAGUNTOWOSETT - b. s. Tassaquanut; Pequot Indian

COBB, ANDREW F. - b. ca. 1853, s. Allen and Sally Cobb, Yarmouth Tribe; res., Yarmouth, Ma.

COBB, DEBORAH JANE - b. ca. 1858, d. Samuel and Polly Cobb,Yarmouth Tribe; res., Barnstable, Ma.

COBB, EDWARD - b. ca.1845, s. Samuel and Polly Cobb, Yarmouth Tribe; res., Barnstable, Ma.

COBB, ELIZABETH - b. ca. 1853, d. Samuel and Polly Cobb, Yarmouth Tribe; res., Barnstable, Ma.

COBB, EMILY TAYLOR - b. ca. 1851, d. Samuel and Polly Cobb, Yarmouth Tribe; res., Barnstable, Ma.

COBB, HENRY ALLEN - b. ca. 1850, s. Allen and Sally Cobb, Yarmouth Tribe; res., Yarmouth, Ma.

COBB, JOHN BLACKFORD - b. ca. 1859, s. Samuel and Polly Cobb,Yarmouth Tribe; Barnstable, Ma.

COBB, MARY CAROLINE - b. ca. 1846, d. Samuel and Polly Cobb, Yarmouth Tribe; Barnstable, Ma.

COBB, SARAH ELIZABETH - b. ca. 1858, d.Allen and Sally Cobb, Yarmouth Tribe; res., Yarmouth, Ma.

COBB, SUSAN TAYLOR - b. ca. 1854, d. Samuel and Polly Cobb, Yarmouth Tribe; res., Barnstable, Ma.

BIRTHS

COCHEATT, COHEAHS, QUOCHEETS, DANIEL - b. ca. 1702, Pequot Tribe, Groton, Ct.

COCHEGAN, COCHEGION, SOLOMON - b. ca. 1735, Mohegan Tribe, Mohegan, Ct.

COHOIZEE, EPHRAIM - b. ca. 1701, King Ninegret Tribe, R.I.

COHOIZEE, JOSEPH - b. ca. 1691, King Ninegret Tribe, R.I.

COHOIZE, TOBY - b. ca. 1671; King Ninegret Tribe, R.I.

COLE, JOHN A. - b. ca. 1843, Gay Head, Ma., s. Fanny Cole of Gay Head, Ma.

COLE, THIRZA R. - b. ca. 1848, Gay Head, Ma., of Fanny Cole, Gay Head, Ma.

COMMUCK, ALICE E. - b. June 12, 1851, d.Thomas and Hannah (Abner) Commuck, Brothertown, NY

COMMUCK, ALZUMA - b. Nov.14, 1832, of Thomas and Hannah (Abner) Commuck, Brothertown, NY

COMMUCK, BERTHA - b. Sept. 8, 1848, d. Thomas and Hannah (Abner) Commuck, Brothertown, NY

COMMUCK, HELEN - b. Aug. 4, 1844, d. Thomas and Hannah (Abner) Commuck, Brothertown, NY

COMMUCK, OMER PASHA - b. May 25, 1854, s. Thomas and Hannah (Abner) Commuck, Brothertown, NY

COMMUCK, SARAH PRENTISS - b. April 12, 1838, d. Thomas and Hannah (Abner) Commuck, Brothertown, NY

COMMUCK, THERESA - b. Sept 29, 1846, d. Thomas and Hannah (Abner) Commuck, Brothertown, NY

COMMUCK, COMMACK, THOMAS - b. Jan. 18, 1804, s. Joseph of Charlestown, R.I.

COMMUCK, VICTORIA - b. June 11, 1842, d. Thomas and Hannah (Abner) Commuck, Brothertown, NY

COMMUCK, WORTHINGTON - b. Aug. 31, 1840, s. Thomas and Hannah (Abner) Commuck, Brothertown, NY

CONE, ANNIE - b. 1860, Mar. 21, Providence, R.I., d. Edward S. Cone

CONE, EDWARD S. - b. ca. 1822, Mar. 3, s. John F. Cone; res., Wakefield, R.I.

CONE, ETNAH - b. 1873, June 11, R.I., d. Edward S. and Mary (Richmond, Noka) Cone

BIRTHS

CONE, FRANCIS - b. ca. 1874, Norwich, of Mary Cone, Providence, R.I.

CONE, LIZZIE - b. ca. 1848, Norwich, d. Angelina Rogers; res., Westerly, R.I.

CONE, MARY - b. ca. 1855, Providence, R.I.; res., Providence, R.I.

CONE, SARAH - b. ca. 1858, Providence, R.I.; res., Providence, R.I.

CONET, EZRA R. - b. ca. 1859, s. Rhoda F. and William R. Conet, Herring Pond Tribe; res., Herring Pond

CONGDON, LIZZIE - b. ca. 1848, Norwich, d. Angelina Rogers; res., Westerly, R.I.

CONONCHET - b. s. Miantonomo and wife Wawarme; Narragansett Tribe

CONWAY, CHARLOTTE - b. ca. 1827, Charlestown, R.I.; res., Westerly, R.I.

CONWAY, GIDEON - b. ca. 1866 s. Charlotte Conway of Westerly, R.I.

CONWAY, SAMUEL - b. ca. 1868, s. Charlotte Conway of Westerly, R.I.

CONWAY, SUSAN - b. ca. 1864, d. Charlotte Conway of Westerly, R.I.

COOK, ADA - b. 1860, Jan.21, Gay Head, Ma., d. Simon and Emily (G. Salsbury) Cook; res., Gay Head

COOK, CHRISTINA PETERS - b. 1852, Dec.19, d. Thaddeus and Emily G. (Salsbury) Cook

COOK, FAUSTINA FRANCES - b. 1853, May 1, Gay Head, d. Lewis and Abiah (Manning) Cook; res., Gay Head

COOK, JAMES B. - b. ca.1854, s. William and Susanna Cook, Yarmouth Tribe; res., Yarmouth, Ma.

COOK, LEVI R. - b. ca. 1856, s. William and Susanna Cook, Yarmouth Tribe; res., Yarmouth, Ma.

COOK, LEWIS - b. 1848, Jan.11, Gay Head, Ma., s. Lewis and Abiah (Manning) Cook; res., Gay Head

COOK, MONCILLA - b. 1868, June 22, Gay Head, Ma., of Christina P. Cook

COOK, WILLIAM HARRISON - b. 1849, June 3, Gay Head, Ma., s. Lewis and Abiah (Manning) Cook; res., Gay Head, Ma.

BIRTHS

COOMBS, DANIEL C. - b. ca. 1848, s. Dinah B. and
Oakes A. Coombs, Mashpee Tribe; res., Mashpee, Ma.

COOMBS, DARIUS - b. ca. 1848, s. Dinah B. and
Oakes A. Coombs, Mashpee Tribe; res., Mashpee, Ma.

COOMBS, GEORGE RUSSEL - b. ca. 1846, s. Dinah B.
and Oakes A. Coombs, Mashpee Tribe; res., Mashpee, Ma.

COOMBS, OAKES - b. ca. 1857, s. Dinah B. and Oakes
A. Coombs, Mashpee Tribe; Mashpee, Ma.

COOPER, AARON - b. 1822, Jan. 3, Gay Head, s.
Aaron & Abiah Cooper

COOPER, AARON H. - b. 1857, April 16, Gay Head,
Ma., s. Aaron and Phebe (Pocknet) Cooper of Gay Head

COOPER, ABIAH - b. 1800, Apr. 3, Gay Head, d.
Thomas & Susannah (Talknot) Cooper

COOPER, ABIAH N. - b. 1851, Sept. 16, Gay Head, Ma.
of Aaron and Phebe (Pocknet) Cooper, of Gay Head

COOPER, ABRAHAM F. - b. 1852, Mar. 3, Gay Head,
Ma., s. Zaccheus and Martha R. (Attaquin) Cooper

COOPER, ADDIE - b. ca. 1863, d. Francis Cooper of Norwich

COOPER, ALICE J. - b. 1859, Dec. 25, d. Aaron and
Phebe (Pocknet) Cooper, of Gay Head

COOPER, ANDREW - b. 1859, Nov. 14, Gay Head,
Ma., s. Belinda Cooper of Gay Head

COOPER, BELINDA - b. 1839, July 18, Gay Head, Ma.,
d. Aaron and Phebe (Pocknet) Cooper of Gay Head

COOPER, FRANCIS - b. ca. 1831, Norwich; res., Norwich

COOPER, GEORGE W. - b. 1818, Feb., s. Thomas &
Susannah (Talknot) Cooper

COOPER, GEORGIANA E. - b. 1849, Mar. 4, Gay Head,
Ma., d. Aaron & Phoebe (Pocknet) Cooper

COOPER, IDA - b. ca. 1860, d. Francis Cooper of Norwich

COOPER, ISAAC N. - b. 1857, Jan. 25, Gay Head, Ma.,
s. Elizabeth N. Cooper

COOPER, JAMES F. - b. 1863, Jan.15, s. Aaron and
Phebe (Pocknet) Cooper

COOPER, JOSEPH - b. ca. 1828, Norwich; res.Norwich

COOPER, LOUISA - b. 1811, Gay Head, Ma.

COOPER, LUCINA - b. 1835, Aug. 4, d. Henry and
Mary (Cooper) James

BIRTHS

COOPER, MARY - b. 1784, Jan. 28, Gay Head, d. of Thomas and Mary (Herrie) Cooper; res., Gay Head, Ma.

COOPER, MOSES P. - b. 1865, June 2, Gay Head, s. Aaron and Phebe (Pocknet) Cooper of Gay Head

COOPER, NANCY A. - b. ca. 1853, d. Aaron and Phebe Cooper, Mashpee/Gay Head Tribe; res., Gay Head, Ma.

COOPER, RHODA FRANCES - b. ca. 1852, d. Martha R. and Zaccheus Cooper, Gay Head/ Mashpee Tribes; res., Gay Head, Ma.

COOPER, SARAH - b. 1856, June, Gay Head, Ma., d. George W. and Sarah (Pocknet) Cooper

COOPER, SUSANNAH F. - b. 1854, Nov. 16, Gay Head, d. Zaccheus and Martha R. (Attaquin)

COOPER, THOMAS - b. 1803, May 8, s. Thomas & Susannah (Talknot) Cooper

COOPER, THOMAS GREEN - b. ca. 1837, Gay Head, s. Anna Cooper

COOPER, ZACCHEUS - b. 1824, Feb. 14, Gay Head, s. Thomas & Susannah (Talknot) Cooper

CORSEY, ABBY ANN - d. London and Julia F. (Jeffers) Corsey

CORSEY, COOMBS WASHINGTON - b. 1845, May 23, Gay Head, Ma., of Landon and Julia F. (Jeffers) Corsey

COWETT, ESTHER - b. ca. 1840, d. Jeremiah Cowett, Mashpee Tribe; res., Mashpee Ma.

COWETT, JACOB - b. ca. 1848, s. Samuel and Esther Cowett, Mashpee Tribe; res., Mashpee, Ma.

COWETT, JAMES F. - b. ca. 1843, s. Jeremiah Cowett, Mashpee Tribe; res., Mashpee, Ma.

COWETT, LOUISA A. - b. ca. 1828, d. Jeremiah Cowett, Mashpee Tribe; res., Mashpee, Ma.

COYHIS, COHOIZE, COGHOOISZE, TOBY - b. 1673, Charlestown, R.I., Narragansett Tribe

CRANK, MARK ANTH. HOWE - b. ca. 1859, s. Julia Ann & Thomas M. Crank, Troy Tribe; res., Reservation, Fall River, Ma.

CRANK, MARY ANN - b. ca. 1856, d. Julia Ann and Thomas M. Crank, Troy Tribe; res., Reservation, Fall River, Ma.

BIRTHS

CRANK, RACHEL - b. ca. 1857, s. Julia Ann and
Thomas M. Crank, Troy Tribe; res., Reservation,
Fall River, Ma.

CRANK, THOMAS M. - b. ca. 1839, d. Sarah Crank,
Troy Tribe; res., Reservation, Fall River, Ma.

CREIGHTON, JAMES - b. ca. 1861, s. Martha
Creighton of Providence, R.I.

CREIGHTON, JOHN - b. ca. 1858 s. Martha Creighton
of Providence, R.I.

CREIGHTON, MARTHA - b. ca. 1824, Charlestown,
R.I.; res., Providence, R.I.

CROCKER, BENJAMIN F. - b. ca. 1859, s. Asa and
Jane F. Crocker, Yarmouth Tribe; res., Barnstable, Ma.

CROCKER, JOSEPH - b. ca. 1859, s. Joseph and Emily
Crocker, Yarmouth Tribe; res., Barnstable, Ma.

CROCKER, WILLIAM W. - b. ca. 1857, s. Joseph and
Emily Crocker, Yarmouth Tribe; res., Yarmouth, Ma.

CROSLEY, CAROLENE - b. d. William Crosley

CROSLEY, ELIZABETH - b. 1790, d. George Crosley;
res., Stonington, Ct.

CROSLEY, GEORGE - b. 1748, Pequot Tribe, Stonington,
Ct.

CROSLEY, GRACE - b. d. William Crosley

CROSLEY, KATHARINE - b. 1787, d. George Crosley;
res., Stonington, Ct.

CROSLEY, LUCENETTE - b. 1807, d. Thomas and
Philena Occom Crosley

CROSLEY, NATHAN - b. 1785, s. George Crosley; res.,
Stonington, Ct. and Brothertown, NY

CROSLEY, SEREPTA - b. d. William Crosley

CROSLEY, SOPHRONIA b. d. Thomas; res., Brotherton,
Wisconsin

CROSLEY, WILLIAM - b. 1805, s. Thomas &
Philena (Adams) Crosley

CROUD, ARTHUR E. - b. ca. 1858, s. M. Emeline and
George Croud, Punkapog Tribe; res., Canton, Ma.

CROUD, CAROLINE H. - b. ca. 1837, d. Daniel and
Lydia Croud, Punkapog; res., Canton, Ma.

17

BIRTHS

CROUD, EDWIN - b. ca. 1858, s. Edwin S. and Mary Croud, Punkapog Tribe; res., Abington, Ma.

CROUD, FRANKIE - b. ca. 1861, s. Edwin S. and Mary Croud, Punkapog Tribe; res., Abington, Ma.

CROUD, SARAH E. - b. ca. 1860, d. M. Emeline and George Croud, Punkapog Tribe; res., Canton, Ma.

CROUCH, ELIZABETH N. - b. ca. 1849, d. Eliza A. Crouch, Dartmouth Tribe; res., Westport, Ma

CROUCH, MARY S. - b. ca. 1842, d. Eliza A. Crouch, Dartmouth Tribe; res., Westport, Ma

CROUCH, RUTH A. - b. ca. 1845, d. Eliza A. Crouch, Dartmouth Tribe; res., Westport

CUFF, BESSIE B. - b. 1868, Jan. 3, Gay Head, Ma., d. Melissa Belain

CUFF, GEORGE B. - b. 1869, Oct. 29, Gay Head, s. Melissa Belain

CUFF, HOSEA - b. ca.1840, Gay Head, Ma.of Abiah Cuff

CUFF, LEVI - b. 1819, Feb. 17, Gay Head, Ma. s. David and Mary (Dodge) Cuff

CUFF, MARY - b. 1843, Dec. 3, Gay Head, Ma., d. Jonathan and Hannah (Peters) Cuff

CUFF, NELLIE - b. 1865, Jan. 8, Gay Head, Ma., d. Melissa Belain

CUFF, PAUL - b. ca. 1826, Gay Head, Ma., s. David and Mary (Dodge) Cuff

CUFFE, LUCY - b. ca. 1839, d. Harriet and Samuel, Dartmouth Tribe; res., Westport, Ma

CUFFE, SAMUEL R. - b. ca. 1846, d. Harriet and Samuel, Dartmouth Tribe; res., Westport

CURRICOMB, ABIGAIL - b. 1778, d. Andrew Curricomb of Brothertown, NY

CURRICOMB, ANDREW - b. 1747, s. Andrew Curricomb, Tunxis Tribe; Farmington, Ct. res., lots 120, 121 of Brothertown, NY

CURRICOMB, ANNE - b. 1770, d. Andrew Curricomb

CURRICOMB, ELIAKIM - b. 1780 of Andrew Curricomb

CURRICOMB, ELIZABETH - b. 1768, d. Andrew and Abigail Curricomb of Brothertown, NY

BIRTHS

CURRICOMB, JESSE - b. 1791, d. Andrew Curricomb
CURRICOMB, MOSES - b. 1794, s. Andrew Curricomb
CURRICOMB, THOMAS - b. July 14,1786, s. Andrew
Curricomb
CURTIS, ELIZABETH C. - b. ca. 1850, d. James W. &
Frances E. Curtis, Chappaquiddick Tribe; res.,
Edgartown, Ma.
CURTIS, LOVE P. - b. ca. 1848, d. James W. and Frances
E. Curtis, Chappaquiddick Tribe; res., Edgartown, Ma.
**CUSHAWASHET (WEQUASHOOK, HARMON
GARRET)** - b. s. of Momojoshuck, ancient Nehantic
Sachem
CUSSENS, DANIEL - b. s. John Quassons (Cussens),
Indian Preacher; Tom's Neck, Chatham, Ma.
CUSSENS, DAVID - b. s. Samuel Quason; great grandson
of Mattaquason, Sachem of Monemoy, Chatham, Ma.
CUSSENS, EBENEZER - b. s. John Quassons (Cussens),
Indian Preacher; Tom's Neck, Chatham, Ma.
CUTLER, BENJAMIN F. - b. ca. 1844, s. Hannah Q.
Cutler, Dartmouth Tribe; res., Stoughton, Ma.
CUTLER, CAROLINE - b. ca. 1842, d. Hannah Q.
Cutler, Dartmouth Tribe; res., Stoughton, Ma.
DANZELL, ALONZO S. - b. ca. 1856, s. Christopher &
Deborah Danzell, Herring Pond Tribe; res., New
Bedford, Ma.
DANZELL, ELLA MELISSA - b. ca. 1858, d.
Christopher and Deborah Danzell, Herring Pond Tribe;
res., New Bedford,Ma.
DANZELL, EVA F. - b. ca. 1859, d. Christopher and
Deborah Danzell, Herring Pond Tribe; res., New
Bedford, Ma.
DANZELL, ROSETTA - b. ca. 1861, d. Christopher &
Deborah Danzell, Herring Pond Tribe; res., New
Bedford, Ma.
DAVID, ALEXANDER - b. ca. 1845, s. George and
Louisa David, Gay Head Tribe; res., Gay Head, Ma.
DAVID, PRUDENCE - b. ca. 1850, d. George and
Louisa David, Gay Head Tribe; res., Gay Head, Ma.

BIRTHS

DAVID, JOHNSON P. - b. 1866, Jan.23, Gay Head, Ma. s. Alexander and Ann J. (Madison) David

DAVID, ROSANNA GERSHOM - b. 1839, April 25, Gay Head, Ma., d. George David and Louisa (Cooper) David

DAVID, SARAH ASHER - b. 1867, Aug. 5, Gay Head, Ma., d. Alexander and Ann J. (Madison) David

DEGRASSE, ELBINA A. - b. ca. 1858, d. Lucinda C. and James W. DeGrass, Christiantown Tribe, Christiantown, Ma.

DEGRASSE, JAMES HENRY - b. ca. 1854, s. Lucinda C. and James W. DeGrass, Christiantown Tribe; res., Christiantown, Ma.

DEGRASSE, LYDIA L. - b. ca. 1842, d. Lucinda C. and James W. DeGrass, Christiantown Tribe, Christiantown, Ma.

DEMING, ALICE J. - b. ca. 1847, d. Mary A. and Daniel Deming, Gay Head Tribe; res., New Bedford, Ma.

DEMING, ANGELINE C. - b. ca. 1855, d. Mary A. and Daniel Deming, Gay Head Tribe; res., New Bedford, Ma.

DEMING, CHARLES W. - b. ca. 1845, s. Mary A. and Daniel Deming, Gay Head Tribe; res., New Bedford, Ma.

DEMING, DANIEL Jr. - b. ca. 1849, s. Mary A. and Daniel Deming , Gay Head Tribe; res., New Bedford, Ma.

DEMING, DYER W. - b. ca. 1852, s. Mary A. and Daniel Deming, Gay Head Tribe; res., New Bedford, Ma.

DENISON, JAMES W. - b. ca. 1838, s. James W. and Sarah Denison, Herring Pond Tribe; res., Nantucket Island, Ma.

DENISON, JOHN M. - b. ca. 1832, s. James W. and Sarah Denison, Herring Pond Tribe; res., Nantucket Island, Ma

DENISON, SUSAN S. - b. ca.1836, d. James W. and Sarah Denison, Herring Pond Tribe; res., Nantucket Island, Ma.

DENISON, WILLIAM H. - b. ca. 1843, s. James W. and Sarah Denison, Herring Pond Tribe; res., Nantucket Island, Ma.

DIAMOND, JAMES - b. 1825, May 10, Waterford, NY, s. Thomas and Rachel (Fey) Diamond

BIRTHS

DIAMOND, RACHEL - b. 1857, June 5, d. James and Abiah (Manning) Diamond

DIAMOND, ROSETTA ELLIS - b. 1862, July 15, Gay Head, Ma. d. James and Abiah (Manning) Diamond

DICK, ADELINE - b. d. Paul & Hannah (Fowler) Dick

DICK, ALEXANDER - b. s. Paul & Hannah (Fowler) Dick

DICK, ALONZO DAVID - b. Brothertown, N.Y., s. Paul & Hannah (Fowler) Dick

DICK, DAVID - b. Oct. 24, 1824, Brothertown, NY, s. Elkanah Dick

DICK, EDGAR MORRIS - b. Oct. 28, 1843, Brothertown, Wis., s. Nathan Crosley and Eunice (Johnson) Dick

DICK, ELLEN - b. d. Isaac & Hannah (Fowler) Dick

DICK, ELKANAH - b. 1789, Charlestown, R.I., s. William and Hannah (Potter) Dick; res., lot 31, Brothertown, NY

DICK, EUNICE - b. d. Paul and Hannah (Fowler) Dick

DICK, HARRIET - b. d. Alexander & Samantha (Seketer) Dick

DICK, ISAAC - b. 1804, Brothertown, NY, s. Isaac and Cynthia (Brown) Dick

DICK, JACOB - b. 1787, s. Isaac and Cynthia (Brown) Dick; res., lot 60, Brothertown, NY

DICK, LATON - b. July 14, 1797, s. William and Hannah (Potter) Dick

DICK, LUCIUS C. - b. s. Alexander & Samantha (Seketer) Dick

DICK, NATHAN CROSLEY - b. Feb. 8, 1820, Brothertown, NY, s. William Dick

DICK, SOPHIA - b. d. Paul & Hannah (Fowler) Dick (Richard)

DICK, THOMAS - b. Charlestown, R.I.; res., lot 27, Brothertown, NY

DICK, WILLIAM - b. ca. 1755, Charlestown, R.I.; res., lot 135, Brothertown, NY

DICK, WILLIAM - b. Feb. 16, 1786, Charlestown, R.I., s. William Dick; res. lot 131, Brothertown, Wis.

DIVINE, ABIAH T. - b. ca. 1849, d. John Divine, Gay Head Tribe; res., Gay Head, Ma.

BIRTHS

DIVINE, AVIS A. - b. ca. 1842, of John Divine, Gay Head Tribe; res., Gay Head, Ma

DIVINE, C. FREDERICK - b. 1869, Jan. 27, Gay Head, Ma., s. Patrick and Louisa (Pocknet) Divine

DIVINE, GRAFTON EARLE - b. 1859, July 11, s. Patrick and Louisa (Pocknet) Divine

DIVINE, HANNAH C. - b. 1850, Sept. 27, d. Patrick and Louisa (Pocknet) Divine

DIVINE, IDA MAY - b. 1861, June 20, Gay Head, Ma., d. Patrick and Louisa (Pocknet) Divine

DIVINE, JEANETTA GRACIA - b. 1864, June 17, d. Patrick and Louisa (Pocknet) Divine

DIVINE, JOHN Jr. - b. ca. 1835, Gay Head, Ma.,s. John Divine and Parnell (Jeffers)

DIVINE, LOUISA - b. 1867, Jan.20, d. Patrick and Louisa (Pocknet) Divine

DIVINE, MERCY ANN - b. 1848, May 10, Gay Head, d. Patrick and Louisa (Pocknet) Divine

DIVINE, PARNELL - b. 1853, April 25, Gay Head, Ma., d. John and Parnell (Jeffers) Divine

DIVINE, PATRICK LAWRENCE - b. 1854, April 29, of Patrick and Louisa (Pocknet) Divine

DIVINE, SIMON JOHNSON - b. 1857, Feb. 11, s. Patrick and Louisa (Pocknet) Divine

DODGE, BETSEY - b. 1786, May 24, Gay Head, Ma., d. Henry and Abigail (Occouch) Dodge

DURFEE, ELISHA, ADDIE - b. ca. 1858, d. James Francis and Maria Elisha, Punkapog Tribe; res., Boston, Ma.

DURFEE, JAMES - b. ca. 1835, s. William and Harriet M. L. Elisha, Punkapog Tribe; res., Boston, Ma.

DURFEE, JAMES F. Jr. - b. ca. 1860, s. James Francis and Maria Elisha, Punkapog Tribe; res., Boston, Ma.

DURFEE, JOSEPH - b. ca. 1840, s. William and Harriet M. L. Elisha, Punkapog Tribe; res., Boston, Ma.

DURFEE, MAHALA - b. 1812, d. Mary (Mingo) and Charles Durfee; granddaughter to Isaac Ompany and Ann Mingo; Fall River, Ma., Troy Tribe

BIRTHS

DURFEE, PATIENCE - b. d. Mary (Mingo) and Charles
Durfee; granddaughter to Isaac Ompany and Ann
Mingo; Fall River; Ma., Troy Tribe

DURFEE, RHODA - b. d. Mary (Mingo) and Charles
Durfee; granddaughter to Isaac Ompany and Ann
Mingo; Troy Tribe; Fall River, Ma.

DURFEE, WILLIAM - b. ca. 1830, s. William and Harriet
M. L. Elisha, Punkapog Tribe; res., Boston, Ma.

FAIRWEATHER, CHARLES H - b. ca. 1853 d. Hannah
Fairweather of South Kingstown, R.I.

FAIRWEATHER, DAVID - b. ca. 1858, s. Nancy Ann
Fairweather of R.I.

FAIRWEATHER, EDWARD - b. ca. 1864 s. Hannah
Fairweather of South Kingstown, R.I.

FAIRWEATHER, EDWARD - b. ca. 1822, res., New
Bedford, Ma.

FAIRWEATHER, HANNAH - b. ca. 1833, Charlestown,
R.I.; res., South Kingstown, R.I.

FAIRWEATHER, JAMES W. - b. 1855, s. Hannah
Fairweather of South Kingstown, R.I.

FAIRWEATHER, NANCY ANN - b. ca. 1828,
Charlestown, R.I.; res., Kingston, R.I.

FAIRWEATHER, SUMNER - b. ca. 1862 of Hannah
Fairweather, South Kingstown, R.I.

FAIRWEATHER, WILLIAM R. - b. ca. 1859, s.
Hannah Fairweather of South Kingstown, R.I.

FIELDS, EMILY R. - b. ca. 1850, d. Philena and Peter
Fields; res., Worcester, Ma.

FIELDS, HANNAH M. - b. ca. 1846, d. Philena and
Peter Fields; res., Worcester, Ma.

FIELDS, ISRAEL G. - b. ca. 1844, s. Philena and Peter
Fields; res., Worcester, Ma.

FIELDS, JOHN E. H. - b. ca. 1848, s. Philena and Peter
Fields; res.,Worcester, Ma.

FIELDS, PHILENA L. - b. ca. 1842, d. Philena and
Peter Fields; res., Worcester, Ma.

FELIX, MERCY - b. d. Assewetough (Betty) and Felix,
Mashpee Indian; Assawampset (Betty's Neck)

FLETCHER, AUGUSTUS R. - b. ca. 1844, Herring
Pond Tribe; res., Herring Pond

BIRTHS

FLETCHER, JULIA A. - b. ca. 1846, d. Thomas J.
Fletcher, Herring Pond Tribe; res., Herring Pond

FLETCHER, MARY - b. ca. 1840, New Shoreham; res.
Charlestown, R.I.

FLETCHER, NATHAN J. - b. ca. 1840, s. Thomas J.
Fletcher, Herring Pond Tribe; res., Herring Pond

FLETCHER, SARAH A. - b. ca. 1838, d. Thomas J.
Fletcher, Herring Pond Tribe; res., Herring Pond

FOWLER, ABBA LORETTA - b. 1843, d. Osamus
D. & Jane (Dick) Fowler

FOWLER, ABIGAIL - b. d. James & Patience
(Dick) Fowler

FOWLER, ALEXANDER - b. s. Jacob & Amy
(Potter) Fowler

FOWLER, BENJAMIN - b. 1774, s. David &
Hannah (Garrett) Fowler

FOWLER, DAVID - b. 1735, s. James & Elizabeth
Fowler; res., lots 105, 119, Brothertown, NY

FOWLER, DAVID - b. June, 1767, s. David &
Hannah (Garrett) Fowler; res., lot 16, Brothertown, NY

FOWLER, DAVID - b. 1813, Feb. 8, s. James &
Patience (Dick) Fowler; Brothertown, NY, lot 100

FOWLER, ELIZABETH -b. 1770, Brothertown, NY,
d. David and Hannah (Garrett) Fowler

FOWLER, ELIZABETH A. - b. 1850, d. David and
Elizabeth (Simons) Fowler

FOWLER, HANNAH - b. 1768, d. David and
Hannah (Garrett) Fowler; Brothertown, NY

FOWLER, HARRIET ADELAIDE - b. 1844, May 9,
d. David & Elizabeth (Simmons) Fowler

FOWLER, HEZEKIAH - b. s. Jacob & Amy
(Potter) Fowler

FOWLER, JACOB - b. 1750, s. James; res., Brothertown, NY

FOWLER, JACOB - b. 1788, s. David and Hannah
(Garrett) Fowler; Brothertown, NY

FOWLER, JAMES - b. ca.1700, Montauk Tribe,
Montauk, L. I.

FOWLER, JAMES - b. 1784, s. David and Hannah
(Garrett) Fowler; Brothertown, NY, lot 100

BIRTHS

FOWLER, JAMES - b. 1795, Mar. 11, s. David and Phebe (Kiness) Fowler; Brothertown, NY; res., lot 103

FOWLER, JAMES D. - b. 1840, Brothertown,Wis., s. William and Mary (Brushell) Fowler

FOWLER, JOHN COLLINS - b. 1817, Sept.19, s. James and Patience (Dick) Fowler; Brothertown, NY, lot 100

FOWLER, LATHROP - b. Feb. 29, 1848, Brothertown, Wis., s. David and Elizabeth (Simons) Fowler

FOWLER, LATON - b. s. of James & Patience (Dick) Fowler

FOWLER, LORENZO DAVID - b. s. Jacob & Amy (Potter) Fowler

FOWLER, LUCIUS SYRENIUS - b. May 10, 1819, Brothertown, NY, s. of Jacob & Amy (Potter) Fowler

FOWLER, LURHEANA (RHENEA) - b. 1776, d. David and Hannah (Garrett) Fowler, Brothertown, NY

FOWLER, MARY - b. 1781, Brothertown, NY, d. David and Hannah (Garrett) Fowler

FOWLER, MARY - b. d. James & Elizabeth Fowler

FOWLER, MARTHA - b. 1793, d. David & Phebe Kiness Fowler

FOWLER, OSAMUS DAVID - b. 1816, s. Rhodolphus & Elizabeth (Dick) Fowler

FOWLER, PARMELIA - b. d. Hezekiah & Fanny F. (Skeesuck) Fowler

FOWLER, PATIENCE - b. 1846, Dec. 25, d. David & Elizabeth (Simmons) Fowler

FOWLER, PHOEBE - b. d. James & Elizabeth Fowler

FOWLER, PHEBE J. - b. 1819, d. James & Sarah (Simmons) Fowler, Brothertown, NY, lot 103

FOWLER, PRISCILLA - b. 1772, d. Ephraim Pharaoh & Phoebe Fowler

FOWLER, PUALLY - b. d. David & Phebe (Kiness) Fowler

FOWLER, RHODOLPHUS - b. 1791, Brothertown, NY, s. David and Hannah (Garrett) Fowler

FOWLER, SIMEON ADAMS - b. May 27, 1819, s. James and Patience (Dick) Fowler, Brothertown, NY, lot 100

BIRTHS

FOWLER, TEMPERANCE - b. s. Ephraim & Phoebe (Fowler) Pharaoh

FOWLER, WALTER A. - b. ca. 1851, s. Mary and Peter Fowler; res., Calif.

FOWLER, WILLIAM - b. 1815, s. James & Patience (Dick) Fowler; res., Brothertown, Wis.

FRANCIS, CORDELIA - b. 1864, Jan.24, Chilmark, Ma., d. Olive B. Francis

FRANCIS, DANIEL - b. ca.1854, s. Catherine, Gay Head Tribe; res., Chilmark, Ma.

FRANCIS, EUGENE - b. ca. 1856, s. Catherine Francis, Gay Head Tribe; res., Chilmark, Ma.

FRANCIS, JANE - b. 1796, Feb. 12, Gay Head, Ma., d. Nathan and Sarah (Amos) Francis

FRANCIS, JEMIMA - b. ca. 1848, d. Catherine Francis, Gay Head Tribe; res., Chilmark, Ma.

FRANCIS, KAWKSKEES - b. s. Francis Joseph Neptune, Chief of Passamaquoddy Tribe; Pleasant Point, Me.

FRANCIS, JONATHAN - b. 1800, Mar.1, Gay Head, Ma., s. Nathan and Sarah (Amos) Francis

FRANCIS, LAWSON B. - b. ca. 1869, Mystic, Ct., s. Almira Gardner; res., Stonington,Ct.

FRANCIS, OLIVE B. - b. 1846, Sept. 27, Chilmark, Ma., d. R. Catherine Francis of Gay Head, Ma.

FRANCIS, THERESA MARY (DELLIS MAHLI) - b. d. Francis Joseph Neptune and wife Mary; Passamaquoddy Tribe, Pleasant Point, Me.

FREEMAN, CAROLINE - b. ca. 1816, Colchester; res., Norwich

FREEMAN, DAVID - b. ca. 1857, s. Priscilla and Tristram Freeman, Deep Bottom Tribe; res., Deep Bottom, Martha's Vineyard, Ma.

FREEMAN, FRANK H. - b. ca. 1859, s. Priscilla and Tristram Freeman, Deep Bottom Tribe; Deep Bottom, Martha's Vineyard, Ma.

FULLER, ALICE - b. ca. 1858, d. Caroline A. and Thomas G. T. Fuller

FULLER, ALICE - b. ca. 1860, d. Salome and David Fuller, Jr.; res., Salem, Ma.

BIRTHS

FULLER, DAVID - b. ca. 1851, s. Salome and David
Fuller, Jr.; res., Salem, Ma.

FULLER, FRANKLIN - b. ca. 1858, s. Salome and David
Fuller, Jr.; res., Salem, Ma.

FULLER, MARTHA JANE - b. ca. 1856, d. Caroline A.
and Thomas G. T. Fuller

GARDNER, ALAMEDA - b. ca. 1859, Charlestown, R.I.,
d. Clark Gardner

GARDNER, AVALDO C. - b. ca. 1862, s. Hannah S.
Gardner of Westerly, R.I.

GARDNER, BENJAMIN - b. ca. 1827, South Kingstown,
R.I., s. Ebenezer and Betsey (Dyer) Gardner; res.,
Providence, R.I.

GARDNER, CLARK - b. ca. 1822, Stonington, s. Maria
and Steven Gardner; res., Stonington, Ct

GARDNER, COURTLAND - b. ca. 1862, Charlestown,
R.I., s. Clark Gardner

GARDNER, DANIEL - b. ca. 1840, Kingstown, R.I.,
s. Mary Ann Gardner

GARDNER, ELLEN - b. ca. 1861, Charlestown, R.I.,
d. Clark Gardner

GARDNER, EUNICE - b. d. Charlotte Potter

GARDNER, GEORGE - b. ca. 1850, Kingstown, R.I.,
s. Mary Ann Gardner

GARDNER, GEORGE C. - b. ca. 1864, Charlestown,
R.I.; s. Maria Gardner, res., Mudville, Ct.

GARDNER, GEORGE W. - b. ca.1867, North
Stonington, s. Eunice Gardner

GARDNER, HANNAH S. - b. ca. 1841, Charlestown,
R.I.; sister to Daniel Seketer; res., Westerly, R.I.

GARDNER, HARRIET - b. ca. 1834, Charlestown; res.
Westerly, R.I.

GARDNER, LUCINDA - b. ca. 1810; res., Stonington

GARDNER, MALBRO - b. ca. 1838; res., Stonington

GARDNER, MARTHA A. - b. ca., Charlestown, R.I.,
d. Clark Gardner

GARDNER, MARY ANN - b. ca. 1810, Kingstown,
R.I.; res., Kingstown, R.I.

BIRTHS

GARDNER, RUSSELL G. - b. ca. 1846, Herring Pond Tribe, s. John C. and Eliza Jane Gardner; res., Herring Pond

GIGGER, ALBERT - b. ca. 1842, s. Sophrona and Daniel Gigger; res., Barre

GIGGER, ALBERT - b. ca. 1849, s. Benjamin and Alice Gigger; res., Barre

GIGGER, AMANDA - b. ca. 1849, d. Sophrona and Daniel Gigger; res., Barre

GIGGER, AUGUSTA - b. ca. 1847, d. Sophrona and Daniel Gigger; res., Barre

GIGGER, ELBRIDGE G. - b. ca. 1841, s. Elbridge and Livona Gigger; Hassanamisco Tribe; res., So. Gardner, Ma.

GIGGER, ELIZA L. - b. ca. 1841, s. Elbridge and Livona Gigger; Hassanamisco Tribe; res., So. Gardner, Ma.

GIGGER, LEVI B - b. ca. 1841, s. Elbridge and Livona Gigger; Hassanamisco Tribe; res., Gardner, Ma.

GIGGER, MARTHA ANN - b. ca. 1841, s. Elbridge and Livona Gigger; Hassanamisco Tribe; res., Gardner, Ma.

GIGGER, WALTER - b. ca. 1851, s. Sophrona and Daniel Gigger; res., Barre

GIGGER, WILLIAM - b. ca. 1845, s. Benjamin and Alice Gigger; res., Boston, Ma.

GODFREY, ALONZO - b. ca. 1846, s. Samuel and Hannah Godfrey, Mashpee Tribe; res., Mashpee, Ma

GODFREY, ANN - b. ca. 1860, d. Samuel and Hannah Godfrey, Mashpee Tribe; res., Mashpee, Ma.

GODFREY, FRANCES E. - b. ca. 1854, of Samuel and Hannah Godfrey, Mashpee Tribe; res., Mashpee, Ma.

GODFREY, JAMES M. - b. ca. 1849, s. Samuel and Hannah Godfrey, Mashpee Tribe; res., Mashpee, Ma.

GODFREY, LYSANDER D. - b. ca. 1844, of Samuel and Hannah Godfrey, Mashpee Tribe; res., Mashpee, Ma.

GODFREY, MELISSA E. - b. ca. 1847, d. Samuel and Hannah Godfrey, Mashpee Tribe; res., Mashpee, Ma.

GOODRICH, SARAH LOUISA - b. ca. 1857, d. Francis & Theodate Goodrich, Chappaquiddick Tribe; res., Chappaquiddick, Ma.

GOULD, BETSEY - b. 1796, Nov. 26, d. Brister & Phoebe (Wamsley) Gould; Ma.

BIRTHS

GOULD, JANE S. - b. 1801, March.12, d. Brister & Phoebe Wamsley Gould

GOULD, JAMES - b. 1819, Sept.15, s. Keziah (Hill) and Camoralsman Gould; Ma.

GOULD, LYDIA - b. 1799, June 12, d. Brister Gould & Phoebe Wamsley

GOULD, MALINDA - b. June 23, 1805, d. Phoebe (Wamsley) and Brister Gould

GOULD, RICHARD Jr. - b. ca. 1851, s. Richard and Sarah W. Gould, Chappaquiddick Tribe; res., Chappaquiddick, Ma.

GOULD, RUBY - b. 1803, May 30, d. Brister & Phoebe (Wamsley) Gould

GOULD, ZERVIAH - b. 1807, July 24, d. Brister & Phoebe (Wamsley) Gould

HALL, LYDIA - b. d. Ruby (Gould) and Benjamin Hall; Ma.

HAMMAR, JOHN - b. ca. 1750, s. James and Margery Hammer of Charlestown, R.I., Narragansett Tribe; res., lot 109, Brothertown, NY

HAMMAR, JOHN - b. ca. 1780, s. John Hammar; res., Brothertown, NY

HAMMAR, JOHN EMERY - b. Sept. 8, 1851, s. Esther (Johnson) and John Crosley Hammar

HARDING, ABIAH - b. 1778, Feb. 17, d. Ephraim & Anna (Pease) Harding

HARDING, ANNA - b. ca. 1775, Feb. 5, d. Ephraim & Anna (Pease) Harding

HARDING, EPHRAIM - b. ca.1748, Holmes Hole, s. of Shubael & Abiah (Luce) Harding

HARDING, EPHRAIM - b. s. Ephraim & Rebecca (Luce) Harding

HARDING, SHUBAEL - b. ca. 1722, s. Harding & Esther (Cottle) Harding

HARDING, THOMAS - b. 1784, Aug. 4, s. of Ephraim & Anna (Pease) Harding

HARDING, WILLIAM - b. 1818, s. William & Abigail (Baxter) Harding

BIRTHS

HARRIS, FANNY - b. ca. 1848, Deep Bottom Tribe, Martha's Vineyard; res., New Bedford, Ma.

HARRIS, LYDIA - b. ca. 1854, d. Benjamin Thomas

HARRY, ARTEMUS - b. ca. 1856, Warwick, R.I.

HARRY, AUGUSTUS - b. ca.1829, Charlestown, R.I.; s. of Daniel Harry of Mystic

HARRY, AUGUSTUS - b. s. Christopher and Clowe Harry, Charlestown, R.I.

HARRY, CHARLES E. - b. ca. 1860, Warwick, R.I., s. Almira Harry; res., Pawtuxet

HARRY, CHRISTOPHER - b. 1747, s. Christopher "Kit" Harry, Narragansett Tribe of Charlestown, R.I.; res., Brothertown, NY, lot 27

HARRY, DANIEL - b. 1807, Charlestown, R.I. s. Patience Harry; res. Prov., R.I.

HARRY, DANIEL, Jr. - b. ca. 1856, South Kingstown, R.I.

HARRY, ELIZA ANN - b. ca. 1863, d. Harriet J. and Augustus Harry of South Stonington, Ct.

HARRY, ELIZA JANE - b. ca. 1868, d. Harriet J. and Augustus Harry of South Stonington, Ct.

HARRY, GEORGIANNA - b. ca. 1864, d. Daniel Harry of South Kingstown, R.I.

HARRY, GEORGE - b. ca. 1859, South Kingstown, R.I.

HARRY, HANNAH - b. ca. 1869, South Kingstown, R.I.; d. Daniel Harry

HARRY, HARRIET J. - b. ca. 1838, Norwich, Ct.; res., South Stonington, Ct.

HARRY, IDA MAY - b. ca.1872 of Harriet J. and Augustus Harry of South Stonington, Ct.

HARRY, LEWIS B. - b. ca. 1854, Warwick, R.I., res., Pawtuxet; brother to Artemus Harry

HARRY, LUKE - b. 1873, s . Daniel Harry of South Kingstown, R.I.

HARRY, LYDIA R. - b. ca. 1866, d. Daniel Harry of South Kingstown, R.I.

HARRY, MARY - b. ca. 1861, d. Daniel Harry of South Kingstown, R.I,

HARRY, MERCY - b. ca. 1805, Charlestown, d. Patience Harry; res., Providence, R.I.

BIRTHS

HARRY, MINNIE GREEN - b. ca. 1873, d. Harriet
J. and Augustus Harry of South Stonington, Ct.

HARRY, RUTH E. - b. ca. 1876, d. Harriet J. and
Augustus of South Stonington, Ct

HARRY, SARAH F. - b. ca. 1853, South Kingstown;
d. Daniel and Mary Harry; res., Narragansett Pier

HARRY, SIMON H. - b. ca. 1863, Warwick, R.I.;
res., Warwick, R.I.

HARRY, WILLIAM H. - b. ca. 1842, Charlestown,
R.I., s. Daniel Harry
of Providence, R.I.

HART, SIMEON - b. 1810, s. Nancy (Brushel) Hart;
res., Brothertown, NY

HASKINS, AMOS - b. 1868, Oct. 10, s. Samuel J. and
Charlotte (Madison) Haskings of Gay Head

HASKINS, BETSEY - b. ca. 1805, R.I.

HASKINS, CAROLINE W. - b. ca. 1851, d. William and
Elizabeth Haskins, Gay Head Tribe; res., New Bedford, Ma.

HASKINS, CHARLOTTE E. - b. 1840, Jan.10, Gay
Head, Ma., d. Samuel J. and Charlotte (Madison)
Haskins of Gay Head, Ma.

HASKINS, ELIZABETH R. - b. ca. 1860, d. William
and Elizabeth Haskins, Gay Head Tribe; res., New
Bedford, Ma.

HASKINS, HANNAH - b.ca.1850, d. William and Elizabeth
Haskins, Gay Head Tribe; res., New Bedford, Ma.

HASKINS, MARGARET - b. ca. 1847, d. William and
Elizabeth Haskins, Gay Head Tribe; res., New Bedford, Ma.

HASKINS, SAMUEL J. - b. 1829, Jan.22, Gay Head,
Ma., s. Amos and Bathsheba (Occouch) Haskins of
Mattapoisett, Ma.

HAZARD, AMY - b. ca. 1802, Charlestown, R.I.; res.,
Westerly, R.I.

HAZARD, FRANK - b. ca. 1850, R.I., s. George Hazard;
res., Ashaway, R.I.

HAZARD, GRACE E. - b. ca. 1879, d. Hannah M.
of Charlestown, R.I.

HAZARD, HANNAH M. - b. ca. 1852, Charlestown,
R.I.; res., Prov., R.I.

31

BIRTHS

HAZARD, HARRY N. - b. s. Hannah M. Hazard of
Charlestown, R.I.

HAZARD, HOWARD B. - b. s. Sarah Hazard

HAZARD, JAMES - b. Dec. 8, 1843, Charlestown, R.I.

HAZARD, JAMES M. - b. ca. 1826, Charlestown, R.I.;
res., South Kingston, R.I.

HAZARD, LUCY - b. ca. 1843, Charlestown, R.I.; res.,
Westerly, R.I.

HAZARD, MERCY ANN - b. ca. 1805, Charlestown,
R.I., d. Patience Harry

HAZARD, MINNIE B. - b. d. Sarah Nichols Hazard

HAZARD, PERRY G. - b. ca. 1837, Charlestown, R.I.;
res., Westerly, R.I.

HAZARD, SARAH - b. ca. 1834, d. Hannah Nichols,
R.I.

HAZARD, WILLIAM E. - b. ca. 1873, s. Caroline
(Holmes) and Perry G. Hazard

HAZARD, WILLIAM H. - b. ca. 1822, Charlestown, R.I.

HECTOR, ELLEN (Niles) - b. ca. 1837, Stonington;
res., Hartford, Ct.

HECTOR, ESTHER ELIZABETH - b. ca.1848, d. Richard
A. and Ann Hector; Hassanamisco/Mohegan Tribes; res.,
Worcester, Ma.

HECTOR, FREDERICK AUGUSTUS - b. ca. 1860, s.
Richard A. and Ann Hector; Hassanamisco/Mohegan
Tribes; res., Worcester, Ma.

HECTOR, GEORGE FREDERICK - b. ca. 1859, s.
Richard A. and Ann Hector; Hassanamisco/Mohegan
Tribes; res., Worcester, Ma.

HECTOR, IDA - b. ca. 1858, d. Richard A. and Ann
Hector; Hassanamisco/Mohegan Tribes; res.,
Worcester, Ma.

HECTOR, LAURA L. - b. ca. 1861, d. Richard A. and
Ann Hector; Hassanamisco/Mohegan Tribes; res.,
Worcester, Ma.

HELM, DAVID - b. ca. 1802, Charlestown, R.I.; res.
Charlestown, R.I.

HELM, ETHEL - b. ca. 1876, d. Thomas A. & Lizzie
B. (Champlin) of Wakefield, R.I.

BIRTHS

HELM, GEORGE A. - b. ca. 1878, s. Thomas A and
Lizzie B.(Champlin) Gardner of Narragansett Pier

HELM, GEORGE H. - b. d. Thomas A. & Lizzie B.
(Champlin) of Wakefield, R.I.

HELM, MARY FRANCIS - b. d. Samuel C. Helm of
Wakefield, R.I.

HELM, MARY J. (Noka) - b. ca. 1852, South Kingstown,
R.I.; res., Narragansett Pier

HELM, SAMUEL C. - b. ca. 1848, Wakefield, R.I.

HELM, THOMAS A. - b. ca. 1850, Wakefield, R.I.

HEMENWAY, EBENEZER - b. ca. 1858, s. Joseph J.
and Fanny A. Hemenway; Hassanamisco Tribe; res.,
Worcester, Ma.

HEMENWAY, EMMA E. - b. ca. 1859, d. Alexander F.
& Emma Hemenway; Punkapog Tribe; res., Worcester, Ma.

HEMENWAY, HEPSIBAH S. - b. ca. 1832, d. Ebenezer
and Emma A. Hemenway; Hassanamisco Tribe; res.,
Worcester, Ma.

HEMENWAY, JAMES H. - b. ca. s. Elizabeth and Henry B.
Hemenway, Hassanamisco Tribe; res., Worcester, Ma.

HENDRICK, SOLOMON - b. s. Capt. Hendrick &
Lydia (Quinney) Aupaumut

HENRY, CHARLES H. - b. ca. 1876. s. George C.
Henry of Westerly, R.I.

HENRY, GEORGE C. - b. ca. 1848, R.I.; res., Westerly, R.I.

HENRY, GEORGE T. - b. ca. 1880, s. George C.Henry;
res., Westerly, R.I.

HENRY, JAMES E. Jr. - b. ca. 1848, s. Jane E. and James
Henry; Gay Head Tribe; res., New Bedford, Ma.

HENRY, MARY ALMY - b. ca. 1846, d. Jane E. and James
Henry; Gay Head Tribe; res., New Bedford, Ma.

HENRY, MARY E. - b. ca. 1 801, d. George C. Henry
of Westerly, R.I.

HENRY, RANZARETTA - b. ca. 1854, d. Jane E. and
James Henry, Gay Head Tribe; res., New Bedford, Ma.

HENRY, WILLIAM HENRY - b. ca. 1850, s. Jane and
James Henry, Gay Head Tribe; res., New Bedford, Ma.

HICKS, MELORA E. - b. ca. 1856, d. Hebron and Mercy
Hicks, Mashpee Tribe; res., Mashpee, Ma.

BIRTHS

HICKS, THOMAS L. - b. ca. 1855, s. Hebron and Mercy Hicks, Mashpee Tribe; res., Mashpee, Ma.

HILL, KEZIAH - b. 1818, Jan. 15, d. James & Betsey (Gould) Hill

HILTON, CLARENCE - b. d. Eliza L. Hilton of Carolina Mills, R.I.

HILTON, ELIZA L. - b. ca. 1848, R.I., d. Ben Thomas of Carolina Mills, R.I.; res., Prov., R.I.

HOLLOWAY, ELLA J. - b. ca. 1858, d. James W. & Susan J. Holloway, Yarmouth Tribe; res., East Sandwich, Ma.

HOLLOWAY, JOSEPHINE - b. ca. 1856, d. James W. and Susan J. Holloway, Yarmouth Tribe; res., East Sandwich, Ma

HOLLOWAY, WILLARD W. - b. ca. 1861, s. James W. and Susan J. Holloway, Yarmouth Tribe; res., East Sandwich, Ma.

HOLMES, BENJAMIN F. - b. s. David Holmes of Charlestown, R.I.

HOLMES, CHARLES D. - b. ca. 1864, s. Francis Holmes of Westerly, R.I.

HOLMES, CHARLES H. - b. ca. 1863, Charlestown, s. Luther Holmes; res., Westerly, R.I.

HOLMES, DAVID - b. ca. 1843, Charlestown, R.I., s. Luther Holmes; res., Westerly, R.I.

HOLMES, FRANCIS E. - b. ca. 1844, North Stonington, Ct; res., Westerly, R.I.

HOLMES, WILLIAM - b. ca. 1841, New York, s. William and Hepsah (Occouch) Holmes

HOPKINS, DUDLEY - b. ca. 1822, Charlestown, R.I.

HOPKINS, LUKE - b. ca. 1815, Montville, Ct.; res., Charlestown, R.I.

HOPKINS, MARY ANN - b. ca. 1826, Charlestown, R.I.; res., Newport, R.I.

HOWARD, CAROLINE ELLEN - b. ca. 1859, d. Catherine L. and John Howard, Hassanamisco Tribe; res., Dubuque, Iowa

HOWARD, CORDELIA - b. ca. 1855, d. Shadrack and Helen Howard, Dartmouth Tribe; res., San Francisco, Calif.

BIRTHS

HOWARD, ELIZABETH - b. ca. 1858, d. Peter and Almira Howard, Gay Head Tribe; res., New Bedford, Ma.

HOWARD, HORATIO - b. ca. 1856, s. Shadrack & Helen L. Howard, Dartmouth Tribe; res., San Francisco, Calif.

HOWARD, JOSEPHINE - b. ca. 1861, d. Catherine L. and John Howard, Hassanamisco Tribe; res., Dubuque, Iowa

HOWARD, LAURA - b. ca. 1860, d. Peter and Almira Howard, Gay Head Tribe; res., San Francisco, Calif.

HOWARD, MARTHA A. - b. ca. 1846, d. Shadrack and Helen Howard, Dartmouth Tribe res., San Francisco, Calif.

HOWWASSWEE, ESTHER - b. 1794, Oct. 8, Gay Head, Ma., d. Moses and Jane (Tallman) Howwasswee

HOWWASSWEE, OLIVE - b. 1800, Aug.30, Gay Head, d. Isaiah & Desire Ompany of Gay Head, Ma.

HOWWASSWEE, ROSABELLA - b. 1832, Aug. 7, Gay Head, Ma., d. Rebecca Howwasswee

HOWWASSWEE, ZACCHEUS - b. 1792, Jan. 11, Gay Head, s. Margaret Howwassee

HYANO, JOHN - b. s. Sachem Ianough

HYANO, MARY - b. 1625, d. John & Mary Hyano

HULL, DANIEL - b. 1819, South Kingstown, R.I..

HULL, ELIZA S. - b. ca. 1851, So.Kingstown, R.I.; res., Rocky Brook

HULL, EMILY L. - b. ca. 1857; res., Charlestown, R.I.; spouse of Daniel

HUNT, ABEE - b. ca. 1853, of Calvin and Lucy C. Hunt, Punkapog Tribe; res., Canton, Ma.

HUNT, EMMA L - b. ca. 1855, d. Calvin and Lucy C. Hunt, Punkapog Tribe; res., Canton, Ma.

HUNT, JOSHUA - b. 1857, s. Calvin and Lucy C. Hunt, Punkapog Tribe; res., Canton, Ma

HUNT, PHEBE F. - b. 1859, d. Calvin and Lucy C. Hunt, Punkapog Tribe; res., Canton, Ma.

JACKSON, AMY - b. ca. 1817, Narragansett Reservation

JACKSON, ELLEN L. - b. ca. 1862, Stonington, R.I.

35

BIRTHS

JACKSON, FANNY L. - b. ca. 1860, d. Hezekiah and
Jerusha Jackson, Mashpee Tribe; res., Mashpee, Ma.

JACKSON, LAFAYETTE - b. ca. 1858, s. Hezekiah and
Jerusha Jackson, Mashpee Tribe; res., Mashpee, Ma.

JACKSON, LAURA ELECTRA - b. ca. 1854, d. Abram &
Martha Jackson, Oneida Tribe; res.,West Brookfield, Ma.

JACKSON, MARY JANE - b. ca. 1856, d. Abram and
Martha Jackson, Oneida Tribe; res., West Brookfield, Ma.

JAMES, ALBERTINA K. - b. ca. 1856, d. George E.
and Jane Elizabeth James, Christiantown Tribe; res.,
Christiantown, Ma

JAMES, ANN - b. ca. 1860, d. Charles W. and Mary Ann
James, Christiantown Tribe; res., Christiantown, Ma.

JAMES, AVIS - b. d.William S. & Avis
(Divine) James

JAMES, CHARLES W. - b. ca. 1823, Christiantown, Ma.;
res., Christiantown, Ma.

JAMES, HENRY G. - b. 1861, May 29, Gay Head, s.
of William S. & Avis (Divine) James

JAMES, LAVINIA V. - b. ca. 1858, d. George E. and
Jane Elizabeth James, Christiantown Tribe; res.,
Christiantown, Ma.

JAMES, WILLIAM S. - b. ca. 1859, s. George E. and Jane
Elizabeth James, Christiantown Tribe; Christiantown, Ma.

JAMES, WILLIAM S. - b. 1830, Mar. 24, Christiantown,
s. Thomas & Judith (Weeks) James

JAMES, WILLIAM WALLACE - b. 1864, Nov. 26, Gay
Head, Ma., s. Wm. Spencer and Avis (Divine) James

JEFFERS, AMOS - b. 1785, Nov. 4, Middleborough, Ma.

JEFFERS, CORDELIA HOWARD - b. 1856, Gay Head,
Ma. Sept. 1, d. Thomas and Lucina James Jeffers

JEFFERS, ELZADA - b. ca. 1859, d. James and Melissa
Jeffers, Gay Head Tribe; res., Gay Head, Ma.

JEFFERS, GILBERT L. - b. 1865, Gay Head, Mar. 26,
s. Wm. and Laura (Johnson) Jeffers

JEFFERS, HENRY HUBBARD - b. 1867, June 5, Gay
Head, Ma. s. Thomas and Lucina (James) Jeffers

JEFFERS, HEPSIBAH C. - b. ca. 1849, Gay Head, Ma.,
d. Wm. and Laura (Johnson) Jeffers

BIRTHS

JEFFERS, HULDAH - b. 1802, Dec., d. Amos
& Bethiah (Cooper) Jeffers

JEFFERS, JAMES W. - b. ca. 1834, Gay Head, Ma., s.
Wm. and Laura (Johnson) Jeffers

JEFFERS, JULIA - b. d. Amos & Bethiah (Cooper) Jeffers

JEFFERS, LOUISA D. - b. 1862, Mar. 7, Gay Head, Ma.,
d. Wm. and Laura (Johnson) Jeffers

JEFFERS, LUCINA A. - b. 1863, Dec.26, Gay Head,
Ma., d. Henry and Mary C. (Peters) Jeffers

JEFFERS, LYDIA - b. 1818, Feb 20, d. Amos
Jeffers & Bethia (Cooper) Jeffers

JEFFERS, LYDIA C. - b. ca. 1850, Gay Head, Ma., d.
Wm. and Laura (Johnson) Jeffers

JEFFERS, MOSES B. - b. 1860, April 16, s. Wm. and
Elizabeth (N. Cooper) Jeffers

JEFFERS, SERENA R. - b. 1869, Gay Head, Jan. 28, d.
Wm. and Laura (Johnson) Jeffers   .

JEFFERS, THOMAS - b. 1826, Sept. 15, Gay Head, Ma.,
s. Amos and Bethia (Cooper) Jeffers

JEFFERS, THOMAS CONANT - b. 1854, Jan.16, Gay
Head, s. Thomas and Lucina (James) Jeffers

JEFFERS, WILLIAM - b. 1811, July 25, Christiantown,
Ma., s. Solomon and Love (Weeks) Jeffers

JEPHERSON, ANNA MARIA - b. ca. 1850, d. Cyra and
Patty Pease Jepherson, Natick Tribe; res., Douglas, Ma.

JEPHERSON, APPOLITE - b. ca. 1842, of Cyra and Patty
Pease Jepherson, Natick Tribe; res., Douglas, Ma.

JEPHERSON, CYRA - b. ca. 1840, s. Cyra and Patty
Pease Jepherson, Natick Tribe; res., Douglas, Ma.

JEPHERSON, GEORGE C. - b. ca. 1846, s. Cyra and
Patty Pease Jepherson, Natick Tribe; res., Douglas, Ma.

JEPHERSON, JAMES M. - b. ca. 1845, s. Cyra and
Patty Pease Jepherson, Natick Tribe; res., Douglas, Ma.

JEREMY - b. s. Joseph Mittark; grandson of Mittark;
great grandson of Chief Noatoasaet

JERRETT, ABRAHAM - b. ca. 1824, Gay Head, Ma. s.
Josiah and Sally (Gershom) Jerrett

JERRETT, JOSIAH - b. 1842, Nov. 3, Gay Head, Ma.,
s. Josiah and Olive (Howwasswee)

37

BIRTHS

JETHRO, JOSHUA - b. s. Nickornoose, Nantucket
Islands Head Sachem

JOHNSON, ABBIE - b. ca. 1856, d. Charity Johnson
of Exeter, R.I.

JOHNSON, ABIGAIL - b. d. John and Abigail
(Poquiantup) Johnson

JOHNSON, ALGERNON S. - b. ca. 1844, Chilmark, Ma.,
of Prince and Eliza (Hazard) Johnson

JOHNSON, ALVAN - b. ca. 1860 s. Charity Johnson
of Exeter, R.I.

JOHNSON, CHARITY - b. ca. 1836, Exeter, R.I.,
s. Priscilla Niles Johnson, res., Richmond

JOHNSON, COLLEN BARDIT - b. s. John Johnson
of lot 138, Brothertown, NY

JOHNSON, ELIZA - b. d. Charity Johnson of Exeter, R.I.

JOHNSON, ELIZA ANN - b. 1869, Jan.7, Gay Head, Ma.

JOHNSON, ESTHER - b. 1813, Nov. 10, d.
William & Charlotte (Skeesuck) Johnson

JOHNSON, EUNICE - d. Emanuel & Martha (Fowler)
Johnson of lot 61, Brothertown, NY

JOHNSON, FRANCIS - b. d. Charity Johnson of
Exeter, R.I.

JOHNSON, GEORGE - b. ca. 1844, s. Salome Johnson
of Herring Pond Tribe; res., Herring Pond Plantation

JOHNSON, HANNAH - b. ca. 1857, Hassanamisco Tribe,
d. James J. and Mary Ann Johnson; res., Worcester, Ma.

JOHNSON, HANNAH - b. 1865, Sept. 26, Gay Head, Ma.,
d. Simon and Emily G. Salsbury Johnson

JOHNSON, HATTIE MARY A. - b. 1863, May 23, Gay
Head, Ma., d. Simon and Emily (G.Salsbury) Johnson

JOHNSON, HENRY - b. s. John, res., lot 138,
Brothertown, NY

JOHNSON, JAMES - b. ca. 1832, Hassanamisco Tribe;
res., Worcester, Ma.

JOHNSON, JAMES, Jr. -b. ca. 1851, Hassanamisco Tribe,
s. James J. and Mary Ann Johnson; res., Worcester, Ma.

JOHNSON, JEREMIAH - b. s. Emanuel &
Jemima (Dick) Johnson

BIRTHS

JOHNSON, JEREMIAH W. - b. s. Emanuel &
Martha (Fowler) Johnson; res., lot 61, Brothertown, NY

JOHNSON, JOHN - b. 1774, s. John; res. lot 138,
Brothertown, NY

JOHNSON, JOHN W. - b. 1818, Dec. 28, Brothertown,
N.Y., s. John Johnson

JOHNSON, JOSEPH - b. 1752, April, s. Joseph;
grandson of Manghaughwont, Mohegan Tribe;
Mohegan, Ct.

JOHNSON, JOSEPH - b. 1776, s. Joseph and Tabitha
(Occom) Johnson, Mohegan Tribe; Mohegan, Ct.

JOHNSON, JOSEPH H. - b. ca. 1859, Hassanamisco Tribe,
s. James J. and Mary Ann Johnson; res., Worcester, Ma.

JOHNSON, LEROY AVERY - b. 1867, June 1, s. Simon
and Emily (Salsbury) Johnson, of Gay Head, Ma.

JOHNSON, MARY ANN - b. ca. 1852, Hassanamisco
Tribe; res., Worcester, Ma.

JOHNSON, MARY V. -b. d. Emanuel and Martha
(Fowler) Johnson of lot 61, Brothertown, NY

JOHNSON, NANCY - b. d. William & Charlotte
(Skeesuck) Johnson

JOHNSON, NATHAN - b. ca. 1840, Gay Head, Ma., s.
Prince and Eliza (Hazard) Johnson

JOHNSON, ORLANDO D. - b. s. Nathan Crosley
Dick & Eunice Johnson

JOHNSON, ORRIN - b. 1815, s. William &
Charlotte (Wiggins) Johnson

JOHNSON, OSCAR - b. Brothertown, Wis., 1842, Mar.
28, s. Rowland and Almira (Fowler) Johnson

JOHNSON, PETER - b. 1838, Gay Head, Ma., Oct. 12,
s. Prince & Elizabeth Hazard Johnson

JOHNSON, ROSA - b. ca. 1866, d. Charity Johnson of
Exeter, R.I.

JOHNSON, ROWLAND - b. Feb. 22, 1816, Brothertown,
N.Y., s. Emanuel and Martha (Fowler) Johnson

JOHNSON, ROZETTA C. - b. Sept. 1, 1857, d. John W.
and Rebecca (Abner) Johnson of Brothertown, NY

JOHNSON, SIMON - b. 1794, Aug. 25, Gay Head,
Ma., s. Simon and Hannah (Cooper) Johnson

BIRTHS

JOHNSON, THOMAS - b. s. Charity Johnson of Exeter, RI

JOHNSON, WILLIAM - b. 1822, Dartmouth, Ma., s. Caleb & Mercy (Terry) Johnson

JOHNSON, WILLIAM - b. Sept. 2, 1774, s. Tabitha Occum) and Joseph Johnson, Mohegan Tribe; Mohegan, Ct.

JOHNSON, WILLIAM AUGUSTUS - b. ca. 1860, Hassanamisco Tribe; s. James J. and Mary Ann Johnson; res., Worcester, Ma.

JOHNSON, WM. PRINCE - b. 1850, Mar. 15, Gay Head, Ma., s. Prince and Eliza (Hazard) Johnson

JOHNSON, ZACHARIAH - b. s. Manahawon (Manghaughwont) Johnson of Mohegan Tribe; Mohegan, Ct.

JOQUIBB, ELIZABETH M. - b. 1723, d. Mamohet; great granddaughter of Oweneco, the son of Uncas; Montville, Ct.

JONES, ABBY F. - b. ca. 1858, d. Axcy Jones, Mashpee Tribe; res., Mashpee, Ma.

JONES, ALMIRA B. - b. ca. 1852, d. Axcy Jones, Mashpee Tribe; res., Mashpee, Ma.

JONES, ANN M. - b. ca. 1853, d. Mary H. and Oliver F. Jones, Mashpee Tribe; Mashpee, Ma.

JONES, CAROLINE F. - b. ca. 1853, d. Axcy Jones, Mashpee Tribe; Mashpee, Ma.

JONES, MARY ANN BROOKS - b. ca. 1817, Stonington, Ct.

JONES, MARY S. - b. ca. 1850, d. Axcy Jones, Mashpee Tribe; res., Mashpee, Ma.

JONES, SAMUEL R. - b. ca. 1856, s. Axcy Jones, Mashpee Tribe; res., Mashpee, Ma.

JORDAN, ANTHONY G. Jr. - b. ca. 1840, s. Anthony and Hepzibah Jordan, Gay Head Tribe; res., New Bedford, Ma.

JORDAN, CHARLES B. - b. ca. 1850, s. Anthony and Hepzibah Jordan, Gay Head Tribe; res. New Bedford, Ma.

JORDAN, JOHN P. - b. ca. 1843, s. Anthony and Hepzibah Jordon, Gay Head Tribe; res., New Bedford, Ma.

JORDAN, JULIUS L. - b. ca. 1844, s. Anthony & Hepzibah Jordan, Gay Head Tribe; res. New Bedford, Ma.

BIRTHS

JOSIAH, CHARLES - s. Jeremy; grandson of Joseph
Mittark; great, great grandson of Chief Noataoasaet
JOWON, ELIPHAT - b. 1770, s. Eliphalet and Esther
(Abimelech) Jowon; grandchild of Abimelech; Ct.
JOWON, HEZEKIAH - b. 1778, s. Eliphalet and Esther
(Abimelech) Jowon; grandchild of Abimelech; Ct.
JOWON, JACOB - b. s. Eliphalet and Esther (Abimelech)
Jowon; grandchild of Abimelech; Ct.
JOWON, JONA - b. s. Eliphalet and Esther (Abimelech)
Jowon; grandchild of Abimelech; Ct.
KANCAMAGUS (JOHN HOGKINS) - b. s. Passaconaway;
res., Fort Worombo, Banks of Amariscoggin River, NH
KEETER, EDMUND - b. ca. 1850, s. Aaron and Mary
Keeter, Mashpee Tribe; res., Mashpee, Ma.
KEETER, J. JAMES - b. ca. 1840, s. Aaron and Mary
Keeter, Mashpee Tribe; res., Mashpee, Ma.
KEETER, J. SYLVESTER - b. ca. 1846, s. Aaron and
Mary Keeter, Mashpee Tribe; res., Mashpee, Ma.
KEETER, LORENZO - b. ca. 1852, s. Aaron and Mary
Keeter, Mashpee Tribe; res., Mashpee, Ma.
KENNEDY, SARAH - b. ca. 1861, d. John and Hepzibah
Kennedy, Mashpee Tribe; res., Mashpee, Ma.
LANG, ELLEN - b. ca. d. James M. and Sarah Ann Lang,
Dartmouth Tribe; res., Rochester, Ma.
LANG, JOSEPH - b. ca. 1845, s. James M. and Sarah
Ann Lang, Dartmouth Tribe; Dartmouth Tribe; res.,
Rochester, Ma.
LAWRENCE, CLARISSA ANN - b. ca. 1844, Ct.; res., Ct.
LAWRENCE, LYMAN - b. ca. 1836; res., Ct.
LOW, ANN JUDSON - b. 1836, d. Michael & Diana
(Peters) Madison
LOW, CHARLES B. - b. 1842, June 15, Gay Head, Ma.,
s. Michael and Diana (Peters) Madison
LOW, CHARLOTTE - b. 1840, Jan. 10, d. Michael & Diana
(Peters) Madison
LOW, ROXANNA - b. ca. d. Ebenezer and Celia Low,
Mashpee Tribe; res., Mashpee, Ma.
MADISON, ISAAC E. - b. 1845, March 18, s. Michael
and Diana (Peters) Madison, Gay Head, Ma.

BIRTHS

MADISON, RAYMOND B. - b. 1858, Aug. 6, Gay Head, Ma., s. Ann J. Madison

MAMOHET - b. s. Mamohet; grandson of Uncas; Mohegan Tribe; Montville, Ct.

MANNING, ALVIN - b. 1816, May 20, Gay Head, s. of Marshall & Hannah (Talknot) Manning

MANNING, FRANCIS - b. 1870, June 11, Gay Head, Ma., s. Thomas and Rosabella M. (Howwasswee) Manning

MANNING, ISABEL - b. 1856, Aug. 7, Gay Head, Ma., d. Thomas and Rosabella M. (Howwasawee) Manning

MANNING, JOSEPH F. - b. 1866, Feb.3, Gay Head, Ma., s. Thomas and Rosabella M. (Howwasswee) Manning

MANNING, MARTHA ANN - b. 1864, Feb. 24, Gay Head, Ma., d. Thomas and Rosabella M. (Howwasswee) Manning

MANNING, MARSHALL - b. 1846, June, Gay Head, s. Alvan and Roxa (Lowe) Manning

MANNING, MARY MARSHALL - b. 1862, March 10, d. Thomas and Rosabella M. (Howwasswee) Manning, Gay Head, Ma.

MANNING, REBECCA JANE - b. 1860, May 15, d. Thomas and Rosabella M. (Howwasswee) Manning, Gay Head, Ma.

MANNING, SUSAN M. - b. 1868, May 28, Gay Head, Ma., d. Thomas and Rosabella M. Manning

MANNING, THOMAS - b. 1811, Oct., Gay Head, s. of Marshall & Hannah (Talknot) Manning

MANNING, THOMAS E. - b. 1858, June 29, s. Thomas and Rosabella M. (Howwasswee) Gay Head, Ma.

MANUEL, JAMES - b. ca. 1838, s. Albert B. and Lucretia B. Manuel; Punkapog Tribe; res., Lowell, Ma.

MANUEL, LUCY H. - b. ca. 1842, d. Albert B. and Lucretia B. Manuel; Punkapog Tribe; res., Lowell, Ma.

MANUEL, WILLIAM L. G. - b. ca. 1848, s. Albert B. and Lucretia B. Manuel; Punkapog Tribe; res., Lowell, Ma.

MASHOW, EMILY O. - b. ca. 1843, d. John and Hope Mashow, Mashpee Tribe; res., Dartmouth, Ma

MASHOW, ISAAC - b. ca. 1838, s. John and Hope Mashow, Mashpee Tribe; res., Dartmouth, Ma.

BIRTHS

MASHOW, JOHN ALBERT - b. ca. 1845, s. John and
Hope Mashow, Mashpee Tribe; res., Dartmouth, Ma.

MASHOW, MARY F. - b. ca. 1835, d. John and Hope Mashow,
Mashpee Tribe; res., Dartmouth, Ma.

MASSECUP - b. s. Miantonomo and wife Wawarme; great
great grandson of earliest known Ct. Sequin Indian;
brother to Cononchet (Nenunteno)

MATTHEWS, ARSULA - b. Sept. 14, 1844, d. Ransom
and Maria Sampson Matthews of Narragansett Tribe

MATTHEWS, EUNICE C. - b. ca. 1851, d. Margaret Prince
and William H. Matthews, Chappaquiddick Tribe; res.,
Chappaquiddick, Ma.

MATTHEWS, ISIDORA - b. ca. 1859, d. Margaret Prince
and William H. Matthews, Chappaquiddick Tribe; res.,
Chappaquiddick, Ma.

MATTHEWS, MATTHEW - b. ca. 1860, s. Ransom and
Maria (Sampson) Matthews of Narragansett Tribe

MATTHEWS, OLIVER D. - b. ca. 1854, s. William H. and
Margaret Prince Matthews, Chappaquiddick Tribe,
Chappaquiddick, Ma.

MATTHEWS, PRINCE WM. - b. ca. 1847, d. William H.
and Margaret Prince Matthews, Chappaquiddick Tribe; res.,
Chappaquiddick, Ma.

MEEKENUMP - b. d. Musquntdowas and wife Meekenump;
granddaughter of Grand Sachem Tamaquashad

MEEKSISHQUNE - b. d. Sianum & Josiah (Ketcanomin),
Sachem of Tisbury, Ma.; granddaughter of Noquitompany

METOXIN, JOHN - b. s. Capt. Hendrick & Lydia
(Quinney Miller) Aupaumut

MIANTONOMO - b. s. Mascus, Narragansett Sachem

MICHEL, ADDIE FRANCIS - b. ca. 1869, Charlestown, R.I.;
res., Hope Valley

MICHEL, AUGUSTA A. - b. ca. 1850, Richmond, R.I.;
res., Richmond

MICHEL, GIDEON - b. ca. 1847, Richmond, R.I.;
res., Kenyon Mills

MICHEL, JOHN E. - b. ca. 1859, Richmond, R.I.; res.,
Richmond, R.I.

BIRTHS

MILLER, PHEBE ANN - b. ca. 1858, d. Henry and Louisa
J. Miller, Dartmouth Tribe; res., Dartmouth, Ma.
MILLS, ELIZABETH - b. ca. 1848, d. Dorcas Mills,
Mashpee Tribe; res., Mashpee, Ma.
MILLS, JAMES S. - b. ca. 1846, s. Dorcas Mills, Mashpee
Tribe; res., Mashpee, Ma.
MILLS, LEWIS - b. ca. 1850, s. Dorcas Mills, Mashpee
Tribe; res., Mashpee, Ma.
MILLS, OPHELIA P. - b. ca. 1854, s. Dorcas Mills, Mashpee
Tribe; res., Mashpee, Ma.
MINGO, CHARLES - b. ca. 1834, s. William & Olive
(Howwasswee) Mingo
MINGO, MARY - b. d. Isaac Ompany & Ann Mingo
MINGO, SARAH F. - b. ca. 1859, d. Clarissa Mingo, Mashpee
Tribe; res., Holmes Hole, Martha's Vineyard, Ma.
MINGO, WILLIAM C. - b. 1862, Feb. 19, Gay Head, Ma.,
s. Mary C. Jeffers
MIONEAMIE - b. d. Massasoit, Grand Wampanoag Sachem
MITCHELL, ALONZO - b. Sept. 1, 1850, s. Zerviah (Gould)
Mitchell, Fall River Tribe (Troy); res., Abingon, Ma.
MITCHELL, ANN J. - b. ca. 1849, d. Zerviah G. Mitchell,
Fall River Tribe (Troy); res., Abington, Ma.
MITCHELL, CHARLOTTE L. - b. Nov. 1, 1848, d. Zerviah
(Gould) Mitchell , Fall River Tribe (Troy); res., Abington, Ma.
MITCHELL, DELORES B. - b. Aug.31, 1834, d. Thomas C.
and Zerviah (Gould) Mitchell (ChicChewee) Fall River Tribe
(Troy); res., Abington, Ma.
MITCHELL, EMMA - b. 1846, June 2, d. Thomas & Zervia
(Gould) Mitchell
MITCHELL, JANE W. - b. June 17, 1828, d. Zerviah (Gould)
and Thomas C. Mitchell
MITCHELL, JOHN - b. June 17, 1841, North Abington, Ma., s.
Zerviah (Gould) and Thomas C. Mitchell, Fall River Tribe
(Troy); res. Abington, Ma.
MITCHELL, LEVINA - b. June 10, 1830, d. Zerviah (Gould)
and Thomas C.Mitchell
MITCHELL, LYDIA - b. Oct. 21, 1843, d. Zerviah (Gould)
44   and Thomas C. Mitchell Fall River Tribe (Troy); res., Abington, Ma.

BIRTHS

MITCHELL, MELINDA (TEEWALEEMA) - b. ca. 1838 d. Zerviah and Thomas C. Mitchell, Fall River Tribe, (Troy); res,. Abington, Ma.

MOMOJOSHUCK - b. s. Mascus; also known as Wetamoozo; res., Nehantic

MONATAQUA - b. 1613, s. Wenepoykin (Sagamore George) and Ahawayetsquaine

MONROE, GEORGE W. - b. ca. 1854, Bozrahville, Ct.; s. Ellen Hector; res., Norwich

MONTOWOMPATE - b. s. Nanepashamet, Grand Sachem of Massachusetts Tribe

MORTON, ROBERT HENRY - b. 1846, Dec.31, Gay Head, Ma., s. William and Patience (Mingo) Morton

MORTON, WILLIAM - b. 1845, June 11, Gay Head, Ma., s. William and Patience (Mingo) Morton

MOSSUCK, LUKE - b. 1769, Farmington, Ct. s. Daniel Mossuck; res., Brothertown, NY, lot 61

MOSSUCK, SOLOMON - b. 1723, Tunxis Tribe, Farmington, Ct.; res., lot 51, Farmington, Ct.

MUCKAMUG, SARAH - b. d. Peter and Sarah Muckamug

MUMINQUASH - b. 1636, s. Yawatta and John (Oonsamog (Awassamog, Wessomog, Ossamog); known also as Rumneymarsh, James Wiser; grandson of Nanempashemet; res., Natick, Ma.

MURDOCK, KATE L. - b. ca. 1858, d. Charles H. and Mary S. Murdock, Hassanamisco Tribe

MURDOCK, LEWIS FRANKLIN - b. 1860, s. Charles H. and Mary S. Murdock, Hassanamisco Tribe

MUSQUNTDOWAS (MUSWUNTDOWAS) - b. s. Grand Sachem Tamaquashad

NAAHKEHOMENIT - b. s. Naanashquaw (Rebeckah) and Naanishcow (John Thomas)

NAANASHQUAW - b. d. Tahattawan, Nashoba Sachem, Concord, Ma.

NAASHWMENETT, SOLOMON - b. s. Naanashquaw (Rebeckah) and Naanishcow (John Thomas); grandson of Tahattawan, Nashoba Sachem; Concord, Ma.

NANAMOCOMUCK - b. s. Passaconaway; res., area of Mount Wachusett, Ma.

BIRTHS

NANAMPASHAMET - b. 1580; s. Salem, Lynn, Marblehead, Ma.

NANAUHCOWEMETT - b. s. Tassaquanut; grandson of Woimpigwooit

NATTOOTUMAU (HANNAH) - b. d. Cheshchaamog, Sachem of Holmes Hole

NEPTUNE, FRANCES JOSEPH - b. s. Jean Baptiste Neptune, Passamaquoddy hereditary Sachem (Governor) in 1725

NEPTUNE, JEAN BAPTISTE - b. s. Peter Paul Neptune; also known as Bahgulwet, Blunt Tail

NEPTUNE, JOHN - b. 1767, s. John Neptune (Hassaongk); grandson of Orson (Assony), Chief of Penobscots

NEPTUNE, JOSEPH - b. s. Peter Paul; also known as Cancongoes, Old Coucouguash, Kokohass, Barred Owl

NEPTUNE, LOUIS - b. s. Peter Paul Neptune; grandson of Hassongk; known as Colonel Louis

NEPTUNE, PETER PAUL - b. s. Sachem of Passamaquoddy Tribe whose birth was 1650

NEPTUNE, SOCCABESON - b. known as Eagle; s. Peter Paul Neptune also known as Jequevesom (James Vincent)

NEPTUNE, SOCCABESON - b. s. Soccabeson (Jequevesom)

NEPTUNE, SWASSIN - b. Old Town, Me.; of Soccabeson; also known as One Hand

NEVERS, DANIEL - b. 1820, Sept. 4, Gay Head, Ma.

NEVERS, EUNICE - b. 1870, Nov.25, Christiantown, Ma.; d. Ann Elizabeth Nevers

NEVERS, RUTH ELLEN - b. 1868, May, Gay Head, Ma.; d. Ann Elizabeth Nevers of Gay Head, Ma.

NEVERS, WALTER SCOTT - b. ca. 1868, Gay Head, Ma.; s. Ann Elizabeth Nevers of Gay Head, Ma.

NICHOLS, ANTRISS (COOPER) - b. ca. 1811, Providence, R.I., d. Henrietta Jackson, Widow of Wm. S. Nichols; maiden name Cooper

NICHOLS, CHARLES - b. ca. 1878 s. Georgianna & Frank E. Nichols of Providence, R.I.

NICHOLS, FRANK E. - b. ca. 1851, Prov., R.I.; res., Prov., R.I.

BIRTHS

NICHOLS, GEORGIANNA - b. ca. 1848, Thompson, Ct. res., Prov., R.I.

NICHOLS, GEORGIANNA - b. ca. 1876, d. Georgianna & Frank E. Nichols of Providence, R.I.

NICHOLS, GRACE - b. ca. 1880, d. Georgianna & Frank E. Nichols of Providence, R.I.

NICHOLS, HANNAH - b. ca. 1823, R.I.; sister to Benjamin Thomas

NICHOLS, MABEL - b. ca. 1876, d. Georgianna & Frank E. Nichols of Providnce., R.I.

NICHOLSON, ELIZABETH C. - b. 1860, d. Joseph and Catherine A. Nicholson, Dartmouth Tribe; res.,Westport, Ma.

NICHOLSON, PARDON C. - b. ca. 1858, s. Joseph and Catherine A. Nicholson, Dartmouth Tribe; res., Westport, Ma.

NICKANOOSE - b. 1659

NICKANOOSE, ISAAC - b. s.Wauwinet (Pomhaman); grandson of Nickanoose

NICKERSON, ADDA - b. d. Simeon Nickerson, Yarmouth Tribe; res., Yarmouth, Ma.

NICKERSON, CELINA - b. ca. 1854, d. Thomas B. & Amelia Nickerson, Yarmouth Tribe; res., East Sandwich, Ma.

NICKERSON, DANIEL H. - b. ca. 1859, s. Thomas B. & Amelia Nickerson,Yarmouth Tribe; res., East Sandwich, Ma.

NICKERSON, DAVID - b. ca. 1855, s. Simeon Nickerson, Yarmouth Tribe; res.,Yarmouth, Ma

NICKERSON, EDWIN - b. ca. 1846, s. Simeon and Melinda Nickerson,Yarmouth Tribe, res., Yarmouth, Ma.

NICKERSON, ELIZABETH - b. ca. 1851, d. Simeon & Melinda Nickerson, Yarmouth Tribe; res., Yarmouth, Ma.

NICKERSON, ELIZABETH E - b. ca. 1853, d. David and Mary Ann Nickerson,Yarmouth Tribe; res., Barnstable, Ma.

NICKERSON, ELLA B. - b. ca. 1860, d. Frederick E. and Isabella Nickerson, Yarmouth/Herring Pond Tribes; res., Sandwich, Ma.

BIRTHS

NICKERSON, EMMA - b. ca. 1855, d. David and Mary Ann Nickerson, Yarmouth Tribe; res. Barnstable, Ma.

NICKERSON, GEORGIANNA - b. ca. 1858, d. David and Mary Ann Nickerson, Yarmouth Tribe; res., Barnstable, Ma.

NICKERSON, JOSEPH F. - b. ca. 1856, s. Thomas B. and Amelia Nickerson, Yarmouth Tribe; res., East Sandwich, Ma.

NICKERSON, MARTHA T. - b. ca. 1859, d. Simeon and Melinda Nickerson, Yarmouth Tribe; res., Yarmouth, Ma.

NICKERSON, MARY JANE - b. ca. 1850, d. David and Mary Ann Nickerson, Yarmouth Tribe; res., Barnstable, Ma.

NICKERSON, ROBERT M. - b. ca. 1858, s. Thomas B. and Amelia Nickerson, Yarmouth Tribe; res., East Sandwich, Ma.

NILES, ANDREW - b. 1841, s. James & Abigail (Johnson) Niles

NILES, ELLEN - b. ca. 1837, Stonington; res., Hartford, Ct.

NILES, JAMES - b. ca. 1780, Narragansett Tribe, s. James; res., lot 93, Brothertown, NY

NILES, JAMES - b. ca. 1704, Narragansett Tribe, Charlestown, R.I.

NILES, PHEBE - b. d. James & Abigail (Johnson) Niles

NILES, JOHN - b. s. James & Abigail (Johnson) Niles

NILES, SOLOMON - b. s. James & Abigail (Johnson) Niles

NINIGRET, GEORGE - b. s. Ninigret

NINIGRET, THOMAS - b. 1736, s. George & Sarah Ninigret

NOHNOSOO, HANNAH - b. d. Cheesechamut, Holmes Hole Sachem; granddaughter of Wauwinit

NOHNOSOO, JOSEPH - b. s. Cheesechamut (Nickanoose); res., Gay Head, Ma.

NOKA, BENJAMIN G. - b. ca. 1845, South Kingstown, R.I.; res., Boston, Ma.

NOKA, CHARLES - b. R.I.; s. Mary Richmond Noka and Edward S. Cone

NOKA, CHRISTOPHER E. - b. 1861, s. Mary E. (Richmond) and Moses Noka

(Richmond) and Moses Noka

NOKA, DANIEL - b. ca. 1857, R.I. , s. Mary E. (Richmond) and Moses Noka

NOKA, GIDEON - b. ca. 1841, South Kingstown, R.I.; res., South Kingstown

NOKA, HENRY F. - b. ca. 1857, Warwick, R.I., s. Samuel Noka of Warwick

NOKA, JOHN H. - b. ca. 1859, South Kingstown, R.I.; res., Westerly, R.I.

NOKA, JOSHUA - b. Charlestown, R.I., s. Gideon Noka

NOKA, LYDIA - b. ca. 1855, Charlestown, R.I.; wife of John H. Noka

NOKA, NANCY - b. 1815, South Kingston, R.I.; d. Sam Noka, res., Charlestown, R.I.

NOKA, PETER - b. ca. 1808; res., Westerly, R.I.

NOKA, THOMAS F. - b. ca. 1861, Warwick, R.I., s. Samuel Noka

NONATOMENUT - b. s. Passaconaway

NONXPWOMETT - b. s. Tassaquanut; grandson of Woimpigwooit; Ct.

NOOSE, PAUL - b. s. Nickornoose, Nantucket Islands, Head Sachem

NOOSE, WAT - b. s. Nickornoose, Nantucket Islands, Head Sachem

NOQUITOMPANY - b. of Christiantown

NORTHUP, BENJAMIN - b. ca. 1835, s. Alice and Cato Northup, Fall River Tribe (Troy); res., Providence, R.I.

NORTHUP, CHARLES - b. ca. 1836, s. Alice and Cato Northup, Fall River Tribe (Troy); res., Providence, R.I.

NORTHUP, DAVID - b. ca. 1843, s. Alice and Cato Northup, Fall River Tribe, (Troy); res., Providence, R.I.

NORTHUP, EDWARD - b. ca. 1830, s. Alice and Cato Northup, Fall River Tribe, (Troy); res., Providence, R.I.

NORTHUP, JAMES - b. ca. 1833, s. Alice and Cato Northup, Fall River Tribe, (Troy); res., Providence, R.I.

NORTHUP, MERCY - b. ca. 1839, d. Alice and Cato Northup, Fall River Tribe, (Troy); res., Providence, R.I.

NOYES, CHARLES F. - b. ca. 1876, s. Sarah A. Noyes of Westerly, R.I.

BIRTHS

NOYES, JOHN W. - b. ca. 1870, s. Sarah A. Noyes of Westerly, R.I.

NOYES, SARAH A. - b. ca. 1851, Charlestown, R.I.; res., Westerly, R.I.

NUNUMPANOW, DAVID - b. s. Monataqua of Malden, Ma.; grandson of Wenepoykin (Kunkshamooshaw) and Ahawayetsquaine

OCCOUCH, CATHARINE - b. ca. 1810; res., New Bedford, Ma., d. Bathsheba Occouch of Gay Head, Ma.

OCCUISH, PHILIP - b. 1716, Niantic Tribe; Niantic, Ct.; res., Brothertown, NY, lots 100 and 103

OCCUM, AARON - b. 1753, s. Samson Occom, Mohegan Tribe; Mohegan, Ct.

OCCUM, AARON - b. s. Aaron and Ann (Robin) Occom, Mohegan Tribe; Mohegan, Ct.

OCCUM, ANDREW GIFFORD - b. 1774, s. Samuel Occom, Mohegan Tribe; Mohegan, Ct.; res. Brothertown, NY

OCCUM, BENONI - b. 1763, s. Samson Occom, Mohegan Tribe; Mohegan, Ct.

OCCUM, CHRISTIANA - b. 1757, d. Samson Occom, Mohegan Tribe; Mohegan, Ct.

OCCUM, JONATHAN - b. 1725, s. Joshua and Sarah Occom, Mohegan Tribe; Mohegan, Ct.

OCCUM, JOSHUA - b. ca. 1716, s. Joshua and Sarah Occom, Mohegan Tribe; Mohegan, Ct.

OCCUM, LEMUEL FOWLER - b. 1771, s. Samson Occom, Mohegan Tribe; Mohegan, Ct.

OCCUM, LUCY - b. ca. 1731, d. Joshua and Sarah Occom, Mohegan Tribe; Mohegan, Ct.

OCCUM, MARY - b. 1752, d. Samson Occom, Mohegan Tribe; Mohegan, Ct.

OCCUM, OLIVE - b. 755, d. Samson Occom, Mohegan Tribe; Mohegan, Ct.

OCCUM, SAMSON - b. 1723, s. Joshua and Sarah Occom, Mohegan Tribe; Mohegan, Ct.

OCCUM, SAMSON - b. s. Andrew Gifford Occom and Patience; res., Brothertown, NY, lot 19

BIRTHS

OCCUM, SALLY - b. 1784, s. Samson Occom, Mohegan Tribe, Mohegan, Ct.; res., Brothertown, NY

OCCUM, TABITHA - b. 1754, d. Samson Occom, Mohegan Tribe; Mohegan, Ct.

OCCUM, TALITHA - b. 1761, d. Samson Occom, Mohegan Tribe; Mohegan, Ct.

OCCUM, THEODOSIA (DOROTHY) - b. 1769, d. Samson Occom, Mohegan Tribe; Mohegan, Ct.

OCCUM, TOMOCKHAM - b. of Mohegan Tribe; Mohegan, Ct. s. Tomockham (Asheneon)

OCKRY, ADDIE B. - b. ca. 1860, d. George T. and Betsy J. Ockry, Mashpee Tribe; res., Mashpee, Ma.

OCKRY, EUPHRASIA A. - b. ca. 1846, of George T. & Betsy J. Ockry, Mashpee Tribe; res., Mashpee, Ma.

OCKRY, GEORGE C. - b. ca. 1854, s. George T. and Betsy J. Ockry, Mashpee Tribe; res., Mashpee, Ma

OCKRY, GERTRUDE C. - b. ca. 1857, d. George T. and Betsy J. Ockry, Mashpee Tribe; res., Mashpee, Ma.

OCKRY, JAMES A. - b. ca. 1850, d. George T. and Betsy J. Ockry, Mashpee Tribe; res., Mashpee, Ma.

OCKRY, MARTHA C. - b. ca. 1859, d. George T. and Betsy J. Ockry, Mashpee Tribe; res., Mashpee, Ma.

OLNEY, BETSEY - b. ca. 1840, Ct., d. Olive Cross; res., Wakefield, R.I.

OLNEY, CORNELL - b. s. Betsey Olney of Wakefield, R.I.

OLNEY, FREDERICK - b. s. of Betsey Olney of Wakefield, R.I.

OLNEY, HOWARD - b. s. Betsey Olney of Wakefield, R.I.

OMPANY, HANNAH - b.; res., South Meadows, Hartford, Ct.

OMPANY, ISAAC - b. s. Noquitompany of Christiantown, Ma.

OMPANY, NAOMI - b. d. Isaac Ompany; sister to Rachel; res., Christiantown, Ma.

OMPANY, RACHEL - b. ca. 1699, Martha's Vineyard, Ma., d. Isaac and Elizabeth Ompany, Christian Indians

OMPANY, SARAH - b.; res., South Meadows, Hartford, Ct.

BIRTHS

OMPOWANUT - b. s. Noatoaset; brother to Chief Mittark; Martha's Vineyard, Ma.

OWENECO - b. 1640 s. d. Sassacus, Pequot Sachem, & Uncas

PAHPOCKSIT - b. grandchild of Wenuchus and Montowampate grandchild of Passaconaway; grandchild of Nanapashemet; res., Penacook

PAINE, ANNA S. - b. ca. 1846, Charlestown, R.I., d. Prince & Nannie (Stanton) Paine; res., Westerly, R.I.

PANUPUHQUAH, DINAH - b. daughter of Panupuhquah of Monomet

PARKER, CORDELIA B. - b. ca. 1853, Herring Pond Tribe; res., Herring Pond

PARKER, DAVID J. - b. ca. 1857, Herring Pond Tribe; res., Herring Pond

PASSACONAWAY - b. ca. 1555

PATCHAUKER, JANE - b. 1760, d. Thomas Patchauker; res., Brothertown, NY, lot 14

PATCHAUKER, JEREMIAH - b. 1801, s. Jane (Patchauker) and Isaac Wauby

PATCHAUKER, THOMAS - b. Martha's Vineyard; res. Brothertown, NY, lot 14 (Peshauker, Pauheter)

PAUL, AMY - b. 1794, d. George and Lucy Paul; res., lot 23, Brothertown, NY

PAUL, ANN - b. 1785, d. John and Penelope Paul; res. Brothertown, NY, lot 4

PAUL, ANTHONY - b. 1758, s. James and Mary Paul, Charlestown, R.I.

PAUL, BENONI - b. 1787, s. Anthony and Christiana (Occom) Paul

PAUL, ISAIAH - b. 1794, s. John and Penelope Paul

PAUL, JAMES - b. 1782, s. Anthony and Christiana (Occom) Paul

PAUL, JOHN - b. 1792, s. John and Penelope Paul

PAUL, MARY - b. 1790, d. John and Penelope Paul

PAUL, NATHAN - b. 1788, s. John and Penelope Paul; res., lot 136, Brothertown, NY

PAUL, PHEBE - b. 1784, s. Anthony and Christiana (Occom) Paul; res., Brothertown, NY

BIRTHS

PAUL, SAMSON - b. 1778, s. Anthony and Christiana (Occom) Paul

PAUL, SARAH - b. 1780, s. Anthony and Christiana (Occom) Paul

PAUL, SOLOMON - b. 1796, s. George and Lucy Paul; res.,Wisconsin

PECKHAM, ABBIE J. - b. ca. 1842, Stonington; res., Norwich

PECKHAM, ELLA - b. d. Lucius Peckham of Norwich

PECKHAM, JAMES - b. ca. 1820, Norwich, brother of Francis Cooper

PECKHAM, LUCIUS - b. ca. 1816, Franklin, Ct.

PECKHAM, MARY E. - b. ca. 1831, Griswold; res. Prov., R.I.

PECKHAM, RUTH - b. ca. 1869, d. Mary E. Peckham of Prov., R.I.

PECKHAM, WEALTHY - b. ca. 1852 of Mary E. Peckham of Prov., R.I.

PEGAN, EDGAR - b. ca. 1849, s. James M. and Hannah Pegan, Natick/Dudley Tribes; res., Thompson, Ct.

PEGAN, JAMES - b. ca. 1860, s. James M. and Hannah Pegan, Natick/Dudley Tribes; res., Thompson, Ct.

PEGAN, MIDDLETON - b. ca. 1860, s. James M. and Hannah Pegan, Natick/Dudley/Tribes; res., Thompson, Ct.

PERRY, CLARISSA - b. ca. 1854, d. William and Mary Perry, Fall River Tribe (Troy); res., Fall River Reservation, Fall River, Ma.

PERRY, LILLIE H. - b. d. Ezekiel & Sophronia (Brown) Perry of Narraganset Pier, R.I.

PERRY, MARIA ELIZABETH - b. ca. 1858, d. William and Mary Perry, Fall River Tribe; res., Fall River Reservation, Fall River,Ma.

PERRY, PHEBE - b. ca. 1857, d. William and Mary Perry,Fall River Tribe, (Troy); res., Fall River Reservation, Fall River,Ma.

PETAGUNSK - (Cecily Su George) b. d. Wenepoykin (Sachem of Maumkeag) and Ahawayetsquaine; res., Salem, Ma.

BIRTHS

Salem, Ma.

PETERS, AURILLA - b. d. Oliver & Anne Peters of
Brothertown, NY, lot 29, lot 3, part of lot 106

PETERS, CHARLES E. - b. ca. 1878, s. Charles and
Melissa (Conway) Peters, of R.I.

PETERS, ELEANORA - b. 1819, Sept. 7, Gay Head, d.
Henry and Dorcas (Rogers) Peters of Gay Head

PETERS, ELISHA - b. 1792, of George and Euncie
(Wampy) Peters; res. Brothertown, NY

PETERS, FRANCIS - b. 1852, Aug., Gay Head, Ma..s.
Samuel and Sarah(Jeffers) Peters

PETERS, GEORGE - b. 1761 s. John and Elizabeth Peters,
Montauk Tribe, Montauk, LI; res., Brothertown,
NY, lots 118,125

PETERS, JEREMIAH - b. 1795, s. Oliver and Ann
Peters; res., Brothertown, NY

PETERS, JERUSHA - b. 1790, d. George and Eunice
(Wampy) Peters; res., Brothertown, NY

PETERS, JOHN - b. 1787, s. George and Eunice
(Wampy) Peters of Brothertown, NY

PETERS, JOHNSON - b. 1782, Jan. 27, Chappaquiddick,
s. of Samuel & Patty (Johnson) Peters

PETERS, JOSEPH - b. 1850, Dec., Gay Head, Ma., s.
Samuel and Sarah (Jeffers) Peters

PETERS, MARY ELLEN - b. 1866, Dec.17, Gay Head,
Ma., d. Mary C. Jeffers of Gay Head, Ma.

PETERS, MARY JANE - b. ca. 1869, d. of Charles &
Melissa (Conway) Peters; res., Westerly, R.I.

PETERS, MELANCTHON - b. s. Amos Peters;
grandson of Nathan Peters; res., Brothertown, NY

PETERS, NATHAN - b. 1791, s. Oliver and Anne Peters
of Brothertown, NY

PETERS, OLIVER - b. 1765, s. John and Elizabeth
Peters; res., lot 29, Brothertown, NY

PETERS, SAMUEL - b. 1809, Feb. 17, s. Johnson
& Mary (Cooper) Peters

PETERS, SAMUEL Jr. - b. 1840, July 14, Gay Head, Ma.,
s. Samuel and Sarah (Jeffers) Peters of Gay Head, Ma.

BIRTHS

PETERS, SARAH - b. ca. 1871, d. Charles and Melissa (Conway) Peters of R.I.

PETERS, SOPHIA - b. 1817, May 14, d. Johnson & Mary (Cooper) Peters

PETERS, WILLIAM - b. s. John Peters

PETTAGOONAQUAH (SUSANA) - b. d. Wenepoykin (Sachem of Maumkeag)and Ahawayetsquaine; granddaughter of Nanepashemet; res., Salem, Mass.

PHARAOH, BENJAMIN - b. 1790, s. Benjamin and Damaris Pharaoh of lot 124, Brothertown, NY

PHARAOH, EPHRAIM - b. 1747, Montauk Tribe, Montauk, LI; res., Brothertown, NY, lot 17

PHARAOH, PHEBE - b. 1785, d. Ephraim and Phebe (Fowler) Pharaoh, Brothertown, NY

PHARAOH, PRISCILLA - b. 1772, d. Ephraim and Phebe (Fowler) Pharaoh of Brothertown, NY

PHARAOH, TEMPERANCE - b. d. Ephraim and Phebe (Fowler) Pharaoh of Brothertown, NY

POCKNET, ALEXANDER D. - b. ca. 1832, s. Moses and Mercy S. Pocknet, Mashpee Tribe; res., Mashpee, Ma.

POCKNET, ANGELINE - b. ca. 1857, d. Elizabeth and Nathan S. Pocknet, Mashpee Tribe; res., Mashpee, Ma.

POCKNET, CELIA R. - b. ca. 1844, d. Gideon and Mahala B. Pocknet, Mashpee Tribe; res., Mashpee, Ma.

POCKNET, ELIJAH W. Jr. - b. ca. 1856, s. Elijah W. and Phebe A. Pocknet, Mashpee Tribe; res., Mashpee, Ma.

POCKNET, GRAFTON G. - b. ca. 1838, of Moses and Mercy S. Pocknet, Mashpee Tribe; res., Mashpee, Ma.

POCKNET, HENRIETTA - b. ca. 1846, d. Moses and Mercy S. Pocknet, Mashpee Tribe; res., Mashpee, Ma.

POCKNET, JACOB - b. ca. 1840, s. Gideon N. and Mahala B. Pocknett, Mashpee Tribe; res. Mashpee, Ma.

POCKNET, JOSHUA A. - b. ca. 1858, s. Elijah W. and Phebe A. Pocknet, Mashpee Tribe; res., Mashpee, Ma.

POCKNET, MOSES - b. ca. 1841

POCKNET, NATHAN ELTON - b. 1870, May 12, Gay Head, Ma.

POCKNET, OLIVIA - b. ca. 1852, d. Elijah W. and Phebe A., Mashpee Tribe; res., Mashpee, Ma.

BIRTHS

POCKNET, PHEBE - b. 1833, Jan. 8, Mashpee, Ma. ,d.
Moses and Phebe Pocknet, of Mashpee, Ma.

POCKNET, PHEBE E. - b. ca. 1854, d. Elijah W. and
Phebe A., Mashpee Tribe; res., Mashpee, Ma.

POCKNET, RELIANCE - b. ca. 1844, of Moses and
Mercy S. Pocknet, Mashpee Tribe; res., Mashpee, Ma.

POCKNET, SARAH ANN - b. ca. 1843, d. Gideon N. and
Mahala B. Pocknet, Mashpee Tribe; res., Mashpee, Ma.

POCKNET, SUSAN - b. ca. 1841, d. Moses and Mercy
S. Pocknet, Mashpee Tribe; res., Mashpee, Ma.

POCKNET, TERESA - b. ca. 1859, d. Nathan S and
Elizabeth Pocknet, Mashpee Tribe; res., Mashpee, Ma

POCKNET, TRIPHOSA - b. ca. 1848, d. Moses and
Mercy S. Pocknet, Mashpee Tribe; res., Mashpee, Ma.

POCKNET, ZACCHEUS - b. ca. 1854, s. Nathan S. and
Elizabeth Pocknet, Mashpee Tribe; res., Mashpee, Ma.

POMPEY, ANGELIA F. - b. ca. 1852, d. John and Elizabeth
Pompey, Mashpee Tribe; res., Cotoit Port

POMPEY, CAROLINE - b. ca. 1856, d. John and Elizabeth
Pompey, Mashpee Tribe; res., Cotoit Port

POMPEY, CYNTHIA A. - b. ca. 1854, d. John and
Elizabeth Pompey, Mashpee Tribe; res., Cotoit Port

POMPEY, EDWARD - b. ca. 1861, d. John and Elizabeth
Pompey, Mashpee Tribe; res., Cotoit Port

POMPMO, LYDIA - b. d. Attamonchassuck of Potonumecot
Tribe; res., Chaquesett; Harwich, Ma. area

PONIT - b. s. Cheesechamut (Nickanoose), Holmes Hole,
Martha's Vineyard, Ma.

POQUIOM, BEN - b. s. Uncas and Daughter of Foxon;
grandson of Meekenump and Oweneco; Ct.

POQUIOM, BEN - b. s. Major Ben Poquiom; grandson
of Uncas and Daughter of Foxon; Ct.

POQUIOM, ISAIAH - b. Montville, Ct., s. Ben Poquiom
and Ann Ceasar; grandson of Ceasar, Sachem of Mohegans

POQUIOM, POMPI - b. 1756, July 5, Montville, Ct., s.
Ben Poquiom and Ann Ceasar; grandson of Ceasar,
Sachem of Mohegans

PRIMUS, DANIEL Jr. - b. ca. 1835, R.I.

BIRTHS

PRINCE, ALMIRA - b. ca. 1852, Mamattakeeset Tribe; res., Pembroke, Ma.

PRINCE, AUGUSTUS - b. ca. 1838, s. Martin and Esther Prince, Mamattakeeset Tribe; res., Pembroke, Ma.

PRINCE, CHARLES - b. ca. 1832, s. Martin and Esther Prince, Mamattakeeset Tribe; res., Pembroke, Ma.

PRINCE, ELIZA - b. ca. 1833, d. Martin and Esther Prince, Mamattakeeset Tribe; res., Pembroke, Ma.

PRINCE, FREDERICK N. - b. ca. 1859, s. Augustus and Eliza M. N. Prince, Mamattakeeset Tribe; res., South Scituate, Ma.

PRINCE, HARRIET MARIA - b. ca. 1857, d. Joshua and Lucy J. Prince, Mamattakeeset Tribe; res., East Abington, Ma.

PRINCE, WILLIAM EDWIN - b. ca. 1856, s. Joshua and Lucy J. Prince, Mamattakeeset Tribe; res., East Abington, Ma.

PRINTER, BETHIA - b. June 1726, d. Moses Printer, Hassanamisco Indian

PRINTER, ELIZABETH - b. April 24, d. Moses Printer, Hassanamisco Indian

PRINTER, MARY - b. Feb. 1719, d. Moses Printer, Hassanamisco Indian

PRINTER, MOSES - b. Oct. 1721, Hassanamisco Indian, s. Moses Printer, Hassanamisco Indian

PRINTER, SARAH - b. d. Moses Printer, Hassanisco Indian

QUAIAPEN - b. sister to Ninigret; R.I. (Matantuck, SunkSquaw)

QUAM, DANIEL - b. s. Sarah Squamamie; descendant of Chief Massasoit of Wampanoag Tribe

QUAM, ELIZABETH - b. ca. 1774, Barkhamstead, Ct., d. James & Molly (Barber) Quam

QUAM, HANNAH - b. Barkhamstead, Ct., d. James & Molly (Barber) Chaughm

QUAM, JAMES - b. s. Sarah Squammamie; descendant of Massasoit; res., Wethsefield, Ct.

QUAM, MARY - b. Barkhamstead, Ct., d. of James & Molly (Barber) Chaughm

BIRTHS

QUAM, MERCY - b. Barkhamstead, Ct., d. of James & Molly (Barber) Chaughm

QUAM, POLLY - b. Barkhamstead, Ct., d. James & Molly (Barber) Chaughm

QUAM, SALLY - b. Barkhamstead, Ct., d. James & Molly (Barber) Quam

QUAM, SAMUEL - b. Barkhamstead, Ct., s. James & Molly (Barber) Chaughm

QUAM, SOLOMON - b. Barkhamstead, Ct., s. James & Molly (Barber) Quam

QUANAMPOWIT JAMES (JAMES WISER, MUMINQUASH) - b. 1636, RumneyMarsh (Chelsea,Ma.), s. Yawatta and John Oonsamog (Awassamog, Ousamog); res. Natick, Ma., Martha's Vineyard, Ma.

QUANSETT, BENJAMIN - b. s. Quequaganet of Herring Pond Tribe; grandson of Narragansett Great Sachem, Canonicus

QUANSETT, JEREMIAH - b. s. Thomas and Naomi (Menekish) Quansett; grandson of Quequaganet of Herring Pond Tribe

QUANSETT, MATTIAS - b. s. Quequaganet of Herring Pond Tribe; grandson of Narragansett Great Sachem, Canonicus

QUANSETT, THOMAS - b. s. Quequaganet of Herring Pond Tribe; grandson of Narragansett Great Sachem, Canonicus

QUASON, AMOS - b. s. Samuel Quason

QUASON, DAVID - b. s. Samuel Quason, Chatham

QUASON, HANNAH - b. d. Attomonchassuck

QUASON, SARAH - b. d. Mataquason, Monemeoy Sachem

QUEQUAGANET (WILLIAM STOCKMAN) - b. s. Canonicus, Narragansett Great Sachem

QUIANOPEN (SOWAGONISH) - b. s. Tassaquanut; grandson of Woimpigwooit

QUINNEY, CATHERINE - b. d. John Quinney and grandaughter of David Naunauneeknuk; Stockbridge Indians

BIRTHS

QUINNEY, ELIZABETH - b. d. John Quinney and
grandaughter of David Naunauneeknuk; Stockbridge Indians

QUINNEY, ELECTRA - b. d. John Quinney and
grandaughter of David Naunauneeknuk; Stockbridge Indians

QUINNEY, EVE - b. d. John Quinney and grandaughter of
David Naunneeknuk; Stockbridge Indians

QUINNEY, JOSEPH - b. s. John Quinney and
grandaughter of David Naunauneeknuk; Stockbridge Indians

QUINNEY, LYDIA - b. d. John Quinney and grandaughter of
David Naunauneeknuk; Stockbridge Indians

QUOIANIQUOND (TASSAQUANUT)- b. s. Woimpigwooit;
grandson of Woimpeguand and wife, the daughter of
Narragansett Chief

RANDOLPH, JOHN P., 2nd - b. 1865, Jan. 23, Gay
Head, Ma., s. Margaret P. Randolph of Gay Head, Ma.

RANDOLPH, MARGARET - b. 1848, May 9, Gay
Head, Ma., d. John P. and Serena C. S. Swazey)
Randolph; res., Gay Head, Ma.

REBIERO, HANNAH E. - b. ca. 1840, North Stonington

RHODES, ARTHUR L. - b. s. William H. Rhodes of
Narragansett Pier, R.I.

RHODES, LAURA - b. ca. 1852, Norwich, Ct.; grandchild
of George Brester; spouse to Thomas Rhodes

RHODES, THOMAS - b. ca. 1869, s. Laura and Thomas
Rhodes of R.I.

RHODES, WILLIAM H. - b. ca. 1848, Charlestown, R.I., s.
Laura and Thomas Rhodes of R.I.

RICE, CLAUDINE - b. d. Hannah (Noka) Rice of
Charlestown, R.I.

RICE, FREDERICK - b. s. Hannah (Noka) Rice of
Charlestown, R.I.

RICE, GERZELLA - b. d. Hannah (Noka) Rice of
Charlestown, R.I.

RICE, HANNAH - b. ca. 1831, Charlestown, d. John Noka

RICE, ISAAC - b. s. Hannah (Noka) Rice of Charlestown,
R.I.

RICE, LEWIS - b. s. Hannah (Noka) Rice of Charlestown,
R.I.

BIRTHS

ROBINSON, ELECTRA - b. d. Salona Robinson of Clinton, Ct.

ROBINSON, ELIZABETH - b. 1868, d. Sarah A. Robinson of Kingston, R.I.

ROBINSON, GEORGIANNA - b. ca.1818, South Kingstown, R.I., d. George D. Robinson

ROBINSON, PRINCE - b. ca. 1818, Kingston, R.I.; res., Kingston, R.I.

ROBINSON, SALONA - b. ca. 1839, Ct.; res., Clinton, Ct.

ROBINSON, SARAH A. - b. ca. 1820, R.I.; res., Kingstown, R.I.

ROBINSON, WILLIAM F. - b. s. Sarah A. Robinson, R.I.; res., Kingston, R.I.

RODMAN, ABRAHAM LINCOLN - b. 1870, Mar. 16, Gay Head, Ma., s. Abram and Roseanna G. (David) Rodman

RODMAN, ABRAM - b. 1809, Sept. 30, Rhode Island, s. Abram and Mary (Trino) Rodman; Narragansett Tribe

RODMAN, BENJAMIN EPHRAIM - b. 1844, Feb. 18, Gay Head, Ma., s. Abram Rodman and Charlotte (Wamsley) Rodman; Gay Head/Narragansett Tribes

RODMAN, CALEB - b. ca. 1848, s. Abraham and Charlotte M. Rodman, Narragansett/Gay Head Tribe; res., Gay Head, Ma.

RODMAN, ELIZABETH V. - b. 1850, March 9, Gay Head, Ma., d. Abram and Charlotte (Wamsley) Rodman; Gay Head/Narragansett Tribes; res., Gay Head, Ma.

RODMAN, MARY JANE - b. ca. 1843, s. Abraham and Charlotte M. (Wamsley) Rodman; Gay Head/ Narragansett Tribes; res., Gay Head, Ma.

ROGERS, ANGELONA - b. ca. 1811, Ct., wife of Thomas Rogers

ROGERS, HERMAN S. - b. ca. 1857, s. Levi and Deborah F. Rogers, Yarmouth Tribe; res., Orleans, Ma.

ROGERS, JOHN G. - b. ca. 1848, s. Levi and Deborah F. Rogers, Yarmouth Tribe; res., Orleans, Ma.

ROSE, HARRIET ETTA - b. 1860, Feb.12, Gay Head, Ma., d. Isaac D. and Harriet A.(Wamsley) Rose

ROSE, ISAAC D. - b. 1811, Nov. 14, Taunton, Ma., s. Samuel and Ruhamah (Bowse) Rose of Taunton, Ma.

BIRTHS

ROSE, MINNEOLA C. - b. 1852, Nov. 5, Boston, Ma., d. Frances A.Rose

ROSIER, JOHN - b. 1793, s. Silas and Phoebe (Wamsley) Rosier; Ma.

ROSIER, MARTIN - b. 1792, s. Silas and Phoebe (Wamsley) Rosier; Ma.

ROSS, ALLEN - b. ca. 1853, Stonington, s. Betsey (Niles) Ross

ROSS, HENRY A. - b. ca. 1855, Stonington; res. Prov., R.I.

SALNOTE, MAHLI (MARY CHARLOTTE)- b. d. Frances Joseph Neptune and wife Mary; Passamaquoddy Tribe, Me.

SALSBURY, BEULAH - b. 1815, Gay Head, Ma., d. John and Naomi (Accouch) Salsbury

SALSBURY, EMILY G. - b. 1833, Gay Head, Ma. d. John and Abiah (Johnson) Salsbury

SALSBURY, JOPHANUS - b. 1826, s. Abiah Tacknish of Gay Head, Ma.

SAMPSON, MARY - b. ca. 1845, Norwich, d. Angelina Rogers; res., Worcester, MA

SAMS, ANGELINE - b. ca. 1836, d. Jane Sams, Chappaquiddick Tribe; res., Chappaquiddick, Ma.

SAMS, MAZILLA - b. ca. 1834, of Jane Sams, Chappaquiddick Tribe; res,. Chappaquiddick, Ma.

SAMS, SOPHRONIA - b. ca. 1831, d. Jane Sams, Chappaquiddick Tribe; res., Chappaquiddick, Ma.

SASSACUS (TATOMBAM)- b. s. Wipigwooit; grandson of Woipeguand; descendant of Tamaquashad; Pequot Tribe, Ct.

SAUCOAUSO (JEPTHA) - b. s. Wanack-Mamack, Chief Sachem of Nantucket

SAUNDERS, HARRIET - b. ca. 1843, Herring Pond Tribe; res., Herring Pond

SAWAG - b. twin to Nawash; s. Sawash, Ancient Ct. Sachem

SAWWASS, SAM - b. ca. 1662; res., Indian Town at North Stonington, Ct.

SCIPIO, ABRAHAM - b. 1795, s. Samuel and Loty Scippio of lot 21, Brothertown, NY

SCIPIO, CALVIN - b. s. Obadiah and Elizabeth (Fowler) Scipio of lot 13, Brothertown, NY

BIRTHS

SCIPIO, CELINDO - b. d. Obadiah & Elizabeth (Fowler) Scipio

SCIPIO, CYNTHIA - b. d. Obadiah and Elizabeth (Fowler) Scipio of lot 13, Brothertown, NY

SCIPIO, DENNIS - b. 1791, s. Obadiah and Elizabeth (Fowler) Scippio of Brothertown, NY, lot 13

SCIPIO, ESTHER - b. 1793, d. Samuel and Loty Scippio of lot 21, Brothertown, NY

SCIPIO, GEORGE - b. 1795, May 18, s. Obadiah & Elizabeth (Fowler) Scipio

SCIPIO, ISAAC - b. 1789, s. Samuel and Loty Scippio of lot 21, Brothertown, NY; res., lot 50, Brothertown, NY

SCIPIO, JACOB - b. 1791, s. Samuel and Loty Scippio of lot 21, Brothertown, NY; res., lot 97, Brothertown, NY

SCIPIO, OBADIAH - b. 1766; res., lot 13, Brothertown, NY

SCIPIO, PHEBE - b. d. Samuel and Loty Scippio of lot 21, Brothertown, NY

SCIPIO, RACHEL - b. d. Obadiah and Elizabeth (Fowler) Scipio

SCIPIO, RICHARD - b. s. Samuel and Loty Scippio of lot 21, Brothertown, NY; res., lot 64, Brothertown, NY

SCIPIO, SAMUEL - b. 1764; res., lot 21, Brothertown, NY

SCIPIO, SARAH - b. 1787, d. Samuel and Lotty Scippio of lot 21, Brothertown, NY

SCUTTAMPE (KASKOTAP) - b. s. Canonicus, Narragansett Sachem, and wife Quaiapen; (descendant of Tashtampack, Ancient Narragansett Great Sachem

SEKATER, ALICE S. - b. d. Johannah F. and Wm. R. Sekater of Wakefield, R.I.

SEKATER, ANN E. - b. ca. 1876, d. Johannah F. and Wm. R. Sekater of Wakefield, R.I.

SEKATER, CLARENCE E. - b. ca. 1874, s. Johannah F. and Wm. R. Sekater of Wakefield, R.I.

SEKATER, GRACE E. - b. d. Johannah F. Sekater of Wakefield, R.I.

SEKATER, JOHANNAH F. - b. ca. 1847, Charlestown, R.I.; res., Wakefield, R.I.

SEKATER, MARY E. - b. d. Johannah F. Sekater of

BIRTHS

SEKATER, WILLIAM R. - ca. 1847, Charlestown, R.I.; spouse of Johannah F.

SELMORE, SAPPIEL - b. ca. 1810, s. Selmore Frances; grandson of Frances Joseph Neptune Passamaquoddy Chief; great grandson of Jean Neptune (Bahgulwet), Head Chief of Passamaquoddy Tribe

SEQUASSEN - b. s. Sowheag, Sachem of Wethesfield, Windsor, Hartford, Farmington Tribes of Ct.

SESSETIM, ALICE - daughter of Patuspagan, Sanchacantacket Sachem, Ma.

SEWELL, MARIA - b. ca. 1809, Hatfield, Ma., d. Hezekiah and Martha Sewell

SHELLEY, EMMA T. G. - b. ca. 1853, Dudley Tribe; res., Stockbridge, Ma.

SHELLEY, IDA ANGELIA - b. ca. 1857, Dudley Tribe; res., Stockbridge, Ma.

SHELLEY, WILLIAM E. - b. ca. 1854, Dudley Tribe; res., Stockbridge, Ma.

SHERMAN, GEORGE - b. s. William & Nancy Hopkins Sherman

SHERMAN, WILLIAM - b. 1825, Pougkeepsie, NY, s. Nancy (Sherman) Mack; res., Nichols Farms, Trumbull, Ct.

SIANUM - b. daughter of Noquitompany

SIAS, ANN - b. ca. 1871, d. Elizabeth Sias of Hope Valley

SIAS, ELIZABETH - b. ca. 1830, Charlestown, R.I.; res., Hope Valley

SIAS, GEORGE G. - b. ca. 1842, Point Judith, R.I.; res., Hope Valley

SIAS, NELLIE - b. ca. 1865, d. Elizabeth Sias of Hope Valley

SIMMONS, ELIZABETH - b. d. of James & Celindo (Scipio) Simmons of (Simons, Simon), Brothertown, NY

SIMMONS, DANIEL S. - b. ca. 1850, s. Lucy M. and William Henry Simon, Mashpee Tribe; res., Mashpee, Ma.

SIMMONS, EMANUEL - b. ca. 1746; res., Brothertown, NY, lot 104

SIMMONS, HARRIET - b. ca. 1854, d. Harriet (Gardner) Simons

SIMMONS, HERMAN - b. ca. 1862, d. Harriet (Gardner) and Russell Simons, R.I.

BIRTHS

(Gardner) and Russell Simons, R.I.

SIMMONS, ISAAC - b. ca. 1860, s. Lucy M. and William Henry Simon, Mashpee Tribe; res., Mashpee, Ma.

SIMMONS, JAMES - b. s. James , Jan.21, 1821, Brothertown, NY; res. Kaukauna,Wis.

SIMMONS, LUCY L. - b. ca. 1857, d. Lucy M. and William Henry Simon, Mashpee Tribe; Mashpee, Ma.

SIMMONS, MARIA - b. ca. 1853, d. Harriet (Gardner) and Russell Simons, R.I.

SIMMONS, MARY - b. ca. 1865, d. Harriet (Gardner) and Russell Simons, R.I.

SIMMONS, MEHITABLE P. - b. ca. 1853, d. Lucy M. and William Henry Simon, Mashpee Tribe; res., Mashpee, Ma.

SIMMONS, REUBEN - b. 1790, s. Abrahm and Sarah (Adams) Simons

SIMMONS, RUSSELL J. - b. ca. 1862, d. Harriet (Gardner) and Russell Simons, R.I.

SIMMONS, WILLIAM HENRY - b. ca. 1854, s. Lucy M and William Henry Simon, Mashpee, Ma.; res., Mashpee, Ma

SIMMONS, WILLIAM R. - b. ca. 1847, Charlestown, R.I.; res., Wakefield, R.I.

SIMONS, ABRAHAM - b. ca. 1750, Charlestown, R.I.

SIMONS, AZUBAH A. - b. ca. 1859, d. Lucy M. and William Henry Simon; Mashpee Tribe; res., Mashpee, Ma.

SIMPSON, ANN ELIZA - b. ca. 1834, d. Zadok and Sarah R. Simpson, Chappaquiddick Tribe; res., Chappaquiddick, Ma.

SIMPSON, GEORGE HENRY - b. ca. 1846, d. Zadok and Sarah R. Simpson, Chappaquiddick Tribe; res., Chappaquiddick, Ma.

SISSELL, ARABELLA - b. d. Mary (Tuspaquin) and Isaac Sissell; granddaughter of Benjamin Tuspaquin and wife Weecum; descendant of Chief Massasoit (Ousamequin), Wampanoag Tribe

SISSELL, MARY - b. d. Mary (Tuspaquin) and Isaac Sissell; granddaughter of Benjamin Tuspaquin and wife Weecum; descendant of Chief Massasoit (Ousamequin),Wampanoag

BIRTHS

SISSELL, MERCY - b. d. Mary (Tuspaquin) and Isaac Sissell; granddaughter of Benjamin Tuspaquin and wife Weecum; descendant of Chief Massasoit (Ousamequin), Wampanoag Tribe

SISSETOM, BETHIA - b. ca. 1703, d. Oggin (Haukim) and wife, Hannah

SISSETOM, DEBORAH - b. ca. 1709, Sanchekantacket, Ma., d. Caleb Sissetom and wife

SKEESUCK, CHARLOTTE - b. 1790, d. John and Anne Skeesuck

SKEESUCK, CHRISTOPHER - b. 1776, s. John and Anne Skeesuck; res., Brothertown, NY, lot 22

SKEESUCK, HENRY - b. s. John and Hannah Galin; res., Wis.

SKEESUCK, JOHN - b. 1746, Charlestown, R.I., Narragansett Tribe; s. John and Elizabeth Skeesuck

SKEESUCK, JOHN - b. 1782, s. John and Anne Skeesuck; res., Brothertown, NY, lot 77

SKEESUCK, SAMUEL - b. 1772, Charlestown, R.I., s. Daniel Skeesuck; res., Brothertown, NY

SKEESUCK, SARAH - b. 1780, s. John and Anne Skeesuck; res., Brothertown, NY, lot 22

SMALLEY, EVALINA - b. 1863, Jan.18, Gay Head, Ma., d. Samuel and Julia (Bassett) Smalley

SMALLEY, JOSEPHINE IDA - b. 1858, Feb.1, Gay Head, Ma., d. Samuel and Julia (Bassett) Smalley

SMALLEY, LEANDER - b. 1865, June 16, Gay Head, Ma., s. Samuel and Julia (Bassett) Smalley

SMALLEY, SAMUEL - b. 1870, July 22, Gay Head, Ma., s. Samuel and Julia (Bassett) Smalley

SMITH, ABBIE - b. South Kingstown, R.I.; d. John Noka

SMITH, EMILY - b. ca. 1850, d. John Smith, Punkapog Tribe; res., Boston, Ma.

SMITH, FRED - b. s. Abbie (Noka) Smith of South Kingstown, R.I.

SMITH, HARRIET - b. ca. 1849, d. John Smith, Punkapog Tribe; res., Boston, Ma.

SMITH, KENNARD - b. ca. 1849, s. John Smith, Punkapog Tribe; res., Boston, Ma.

BIRTHS

SMITH, ROWLAND - b. s. Abbie (Noka) Smith of South Kingstown, R.I.

SOCKBASON, Mrs. - b. d. Governor Frances Joseph Neptune and wife Mary, Passamaquoddy Tribe

SOSEPSIS, K'CHI - b. oldest s. Frances Joseph, Chief of Passamaquoddy (Joseph, Jr.) Tribe

SOUGONUSK - b. d. Arramamet; granddaughter of Rewen

SOUSOACO - b. s. of Qannochamack (Wannochamack)

SOWHEAG - b. s. Sawag; grandson of Sawash, Ancient Ct. Sachem

SPENCER, CELESTINE - b. 1870, May 24, Gay Head, Ma., d. Francis and Amy (Wamsley) Spencer

SPENCER, FRANCIS - b. 1836, June 9, Christiantown, Ma., s. John Spencer of Cape de Verde and Mary James of Christiantown, Ma.

SPRAGUE, ANGELA MARIA - b. ca. 1861, d. Israel and Sally Maria Sprague, Dudley Tribe; res., Webster, Ma.

SPRAGUE, MARY ELLA - b. ca. 1854, d. Israel and Sally Maria Sprague, Dudley Tribe; res., Webster, Ma.

SQUAMAMIE, BENJAMIN - b. s. Benjamin Squamammie; grandson of Tuspaquin and Mioneamie; great grandson of Chief Massasoit of Wampanoag Tribe; Ma.

SQUAMAMIE, BENJAMIN - b. s. Mioneamie and Tuspaquin; grandson of Chief Massasoit of Wampanoag Tribe; Ma.

SQUAMAMIE, SARAH - b. d. Benjamin Squamame; descendant of Chief Massasoit, Wampanoag Tribe; Ma.

SQUAMAMIE, SARAH - b. d. Sarah Squamamie; descendant of Chief Massasoit, Wampanoag Tribe; Ma.

STANTON, HANNAH M. - b. d. Joseph & Patience Stanton; R.I.

STANTON, HORATIO S. - b. s. Joseph & Patience Stanton; R.I.

STANTON, JEREMIAH - b. s. Joseph & Patience Stanton; R.I.

STANTON, JOSEPH - b. ca. 1862, Charlestown, R.I., s. of Luther Stanton

STANTON, JOSEPH B. - b. s. Joseph & Patience Stanton; R.I.

BIRTHS

STANTON, KATIE - b. R.I., d. Joseph & Patience Stanton

STEMBURG, SALLY A. - b. ca.1 849, d. Thomas
Stemburg, Punkapog Tribe; res., Boston, Ma.

STEPHENS, RICHARD - b. s. Sarah Quason of
Cotchpinict, (Chatham, Ma. area) and Stephen Maskuck
(Wasnechsuk); grandson of Mataquason, Sachem of
Monemoy

STEPHENS, SIMON - b. s. Richard Stephen; grandson of
Sarah (Quason)and Stephen Maskuck; great grandson
of Mataquason, Sachem of Monemoy; Chatham, Ma.

STEPHENS, STEPHEN - b. s. Stephen Maskuck and
wife Sarah Quason of Cotchpinicut, (Chatham, Ma. area)

SULLIVAN, MARY E. - b. ca. 1856, Charlestown, R.I.; d.
of Benjamin Thomas

SUNKEEJUNASUC - b. s. Tassaquanut; grandson of
Woimpigwooit; Ct.

SYLVIA, ELEANORA P. - b. 1851, Oct.28, Gay Head, Ma.,
d. Francis and Eleanora (Peters) Syvia of Gay Head, Ma

SYLVIA, NAOMI P. - b. 1869, Nov.28, Gay Head, Ma.,
d. Eleanora P. Sylvia of Gay Head, Ma.

TAGOWASCE (AARON JOSEPH) - b. Dec.21, 1700,
Dutch Reformed Church, Schenectady, NY

TALBOT, AMELIA - b. ca. 1860, d. Martha Ann and
John T. Talbot, Dartmouth Tribe; res., Stoughton, Ma.

TALBOT, CECILIA FRANCES - b. ca. 1856, d.
Martha Ann and John T.Talbot, Dartmouth Tribe; res.,
Stoughton, Ma.

TALBOT, EMMA F. - b. ca. 1855, d. Lucy and Joseph
Talbot, Mashpee/Troy Tribes res., Randolph, Ma.

TALBOT, JOSEPHINE - b. ca. 1851, d. Lucy and Joseph
Talbot, Mashpee/Troy Tribes res., Randolph, Ma.

TALBOT, LUCY A. - b. ca. 1858, d. Lucy and Joseph
Talbot, Troy/Punkapog Tribes; res., Randolph, Ma.

TALBOT, SARAH J. - b. ca. 1853, d. Lucy and Joseph
Talbot, Troy/Punkapog Tribes; res., Randolph, Ma. res.,
Randolph, Ma.

TARRAMUGGUS - b. s. Sowheag, Chief of Wongunk
Tribe; Middletown, Ct.

BIRTHS

TASSAQUANUT - b. s. Woimpigwooit; grandson of
Woimpeguand and daughter of Narragansett Chief;
Descendant of Ancient Pequot Sachem

TASUNSQUAW - b. d. Tahattawan, Nashoba Sachem;
Concord, Ma.

TATAWAN, JOHN - b. s. Tahattawan, Nashoba Sachem,
Concord, Ma.

TAYLOR, CHARLOTTE - b. ca. 1849, d. Desire M. and
William Taylor,Yarmouth Tribe; res., Barnstable, Ma.

TAYLOR, FRANCIS - b. ca. 1856, s. Margaret and
Francis Taylor, Yarmouth Tribe; res., Barnstable, Ma.

TAYLOR, JOHN - b. ca. 1852, s. Desire M. and William
Taylor,Yarmouth Tribe; res., Barnstable, Ma.

TAYLOR, JOHN - b. ca. 1856, s. Margaret and Francis
Taylor,Yarmouth Tribe; res., Barnstable, Ma.

TAYLOR, JULIA - b. ca. 1849, d. Desire M. and
William Taylor,Yarmouth Tribe; res., Barnstable, Ma.

TAYLOR, SUSAN - b. ca. 1840, d. Desire M. and
William Taylor,Yarmouth Tribe; res., Barnstable, Ma.

TAYLOR, THOMAS - b. ca. 1837, s. Desire M. and
William Taylor,Yarmouth Tribe; res., Barnstable, Ma.

TAYLOR, THOMAS - b. ca. 1855, s. Margaret and
Francis Taylor, Yarmouth

TAYLOR, THOMAS H. - b. ca. 1850, Exeter, R.I.

TAYLOR, THOMAS H. Jr. - b. s. Thomas H. Taylor
of Exeter, R.I. Tribe; res., Barnstable, Ma.

TAYLOR, WILLIAM ALBERT - b. ca., 1846, s. Desire M.
and William Taylor, Yarmouth Tribe; res., Barnstable, Ma.

TERRY, ABIGAIL JANE - b. Dec. 1812, d. Nero and
Abigail (Cooper) Terry, Fall River Tribe (Troy); Fall River,
Ma.

TERRY, MERCY - b. 1778, Assonet, Ma.

TERRY, STEPHEN - b. ca. 1811, Fall River Tribe; res.,
Middleborough, Ma.

THOMAS, ANNIE - b. ca. 1852, Reservation, d. F. D.
Thomas of Providence, R.I., res., Norwich, Ct.

THOMAS, B.F. - b. ca. 1850, s. Benjamin Thomas
of Providence, R.I.

BIRTHS

THOMAS, BELL - b. ca. 1873, child- Samuel Thomas of Westerly, R.I.

THOMAS, CARRIE - b. ca. 1873, d. B. F. Thomas of Providence, R.I.

THOMAS, COURTLAND - b. 1872, s. Samuel Thomas of Westerly, R.I.

THOMAS, ELIZABETH R. - b. ca. 1839, d. William and Mary Thomas, Punkapog Tribe; res., Providence, R.I.

THOMAS, F.D. - b. ca. 1846, R.I.; res., Prov., R.I.

THOMAS, FREDERICK - b. ca. 1860, s. George and Adeline Thomas; res., Roxbury, Ma.

THOMAS, GEORGE S. - b. ca. 1842, s. William and Mary Thomas, Punkapog Tribe; res., Providence, R.I.

THOMAS, GERTIE - b. 1874 d. Samuel Thomas of Westerly, R.I.

THOMAS, HELEN A. - b. ca. 1844, d. William and Mary Thomas, Punkapog Tribe; res., Providence, R.I.

THOMAS, LESTER - b. ca. 1858, s. George and Adeline; res., Roxbury, Ma.

THOMAS, LIZZIE - b. ca. 1871, d. B. F. Thomas of Providence, R.I.

THOMAS, LORENZO - b. ca. 1878, s. B. F. Thomas of Providence, R.I.

THOMAS, LUCINA - b. ca. 1856, d. George and Adeline Thomas; res., Roxbury, Ma.

THOMAS, SAMUEL - b. ca. 1843, R.I.; res., Westerly, R.I.

THOMAS, JOHN, Jr. - b. s. Naanashquaw (Rebeckah) and Naanishcow (John Thomas) grandson of Nashoba Sachem, Tahattawan; Concord, Ma.

THOMAS, WILLIE - b. 1876 s. B. F. Thomas of Providence, R.I.

TIGHMAN, CHARLES F. - b. ca. 1843, s. Eliza and Samuel I. Tighman, Dartmouth Tribe; res., New Bedford, Ma.

TIGHMAN, EUGENE P. - b. ca. 1860, s. Eliza and Samuel I. Tighman, Dartmouth Tribe; res., New Bedford, Ma.

TIGHMAN, HIRAM - b. ca. 1851, s. Eliza and Samuel I. Tighman, Dartmouth Tribe; res., New Bedford, Ma.

TIGHMAN, MARY - b. ca. 1849, d. Eliza and Samuel I. Tighman, Dartmouth Tribe; res., New Bedford, Ma.

BIRTHS

TIGHMAN, WALTER S. - b. ca. 1845, s. Eliza and Samuel I. Tighman, Dartmouth Tribe; res., New Bedford, Ma.

TOBEY, ALPHONSO - b. ca. s. Ephraim and Philena Tobey, Mashpee Tribe; res., Mashpee, Ma.

TOBEY, CORINNE - b. ca. 1857, s. Philena and Ephraim, Mashpee Tribe; res., Mashpee, Ma.

TOBEY, HENRIETTA - b. ca. 1840, d. Leah and Joseph Tobey, Jr., Mashpee Tribe

TOBEY, JEDIDA - b. ca. 1847, d. Leah and Joseph Toby, Jr., Mashpee Tribe; res., Mashpee, Ma

TOBEY, JOHN - b. ca. 1845, s. Leah and Joseph Toby, Jr., Mashpee Tribe; res., Mashpee, Ma.

TOBEY, MARGARET - b. ca. 1839, d. Jedida and Josepth Tobey, Mashpee Tribe; res., Mashpee, Ma.

TOBEY, MARGARET - b. ca. 1859, d. Philena and Ephraim, Mashpee Tribe; res., Mashpee, Ma.

TOBEY, SIDNEY - b. ca. 1856, s. Philena and Ephraim Tobey, Mashpee Tribe; res., Mashpee, Ma.

TOBEY, SYLVANUS - b. ca. 1835, s. Jedida and Joseph Tobey, Mashpee Tribe; res., Mashpee, Ma.

TOBEY, OAKES A. - b. ca. of Jedida and Joseph Tobey, Mashpee Tribe; res., Mashpee, Ma.

TOKOMUS - b. s. Sarah (Quason) and Stephen Maskuck (Wasnechsuk); grandson of Sachem of Monemoy, Mataquason; Chatham, Ma.

TOKOMUS, CYNTHIA - b. d. Peter and Lucy (Tantaquidgeon) Tokomus

TOKOMUS, ELIPHALET - b. s. Peter and Lucy (Tantaquidgeon) Tokomus

TOKOMUS, PETER - b. s. Tokomus; grandson of Sarah (Quason) and Stephen Maskuck(Wasnechsuk); great grandson of Mataquason, Sachem of Monemoy; res., Yarmouth, Ma.

TOKOMUS, SARAH - b. d. Peter and Lucy (Tantaquidgeon) Tokomus

TONEY, GERTRUDE - b. ca. 1858, d. Lucretia and Augustus Toney, Punkapog Tribe; res., Lowell, Ma.

TONEY, FRANCIS - b. ca. 1861, s. Lucretia and Augustus Toney, Punkapog Tribe; res., Lowell, Ma.

BIRTHS

TONTOQUON (JOHN) - b. s. Petagunsk (Cecily Su George); grandson of Wenepoykin and wife Ahawayetsquaine; Great grandson of Nanepashamet; Lynn, Ma.

TOUCEE, AARON - b. 1793, s. Benjamin and Elizabeth Curricomb) Toucee

TOUCEE, BENJAMIN - b. 1765, Farmington, Ct., Tunxis Tribe, s. David Towsey; res., Brothertown, NY, lot 20

TOUCEE, DAVID - b. Aug. 9, 1800, Brothertown, NY; res., lot 87, Brothertown, NY

TOUCEE, JOSEPH - b. 1769, s. David Towsey, Tunxis Tribe; Farmington, Ct.

TOUNTOSHEMON - b. s. Tassaquanut; grandson of Woimpigwooit; Descendant of Ancient Pequot Great Sachem, Tamaquashad; Ct.

TUHIE, JEREMIAH - b. 1768, s. John and Sarah Tuhie, Brothertown, NY; res., lot 8, Brothertown, NY

TUHIE, JOHN - b. ca. 1746, Narragansett Tribe, Charlestown, R.I., s. Joseph

TUHIE, JOHN - b. 1744, Narragansett Tribe, Charlestown, R.I., s. Joseph and Jane Tuhie (Tuhuy,Tuhi,Tohigh,Tohoy); res., lots 11,18

TUPHAUS, BETHIA - b. ca. 1700, d. Wm. and Bethia Tuphaus, of Chilmark, Ma.

TUPHAUS, JOB - b. ca. 1699, s. Wm. and Bethia (Amos) Tuphaus, of Chilmark, Ma

TUPHAUS, WILLIAM - b. ca. 1681, s. Wm.and Bethiah (Amos) Tuphaus of Chilmark, Ma.

TURNER, NATHAN - b. 1863, Oct.1, s. Rachel Turner; res., Plymouth, Ma.

TUSPAQUIN, ESTHER - b. d. Benjamin and Weecum Tuspaquin

TUSPAQUIN, HANNAH - b. d. Benjamin and Weecum Tuspaquin

TUSPAQUIN, JOHN - b. d. Benjamin and Weecum Tuspaquin

TUSPAQUIN, LYDIA - b. d. Benjamin Tuspaquin and Mercy Felix; Ma.

TUSPAQUIN, MARY - b. d. Benjamin and Weecum Tuspaquin

BIRTHS

TUSPAQUIN, MARY - b. d. William Tuspaquin (Soquantamuck)

TUSPAQUIN, WILLIAM (SOQUANTAMUK) - b. s. Mioneamie and Tuspaquin; grandson of Chief Massasoit of Wampanoag Tribe

UNANUGUAOSET - b. s. Passaconaway of Pennacook, NH

UNCAS - b.1588, s. Meekenump and Oweneco; grandson of Musqundtowas

UNCAS, JOHN - b. s. Uncas and Daughter of Sassacus; Mohegan Tribe

UNCAS, JOHN - b. s. John Uncas; grandson of Uncas; great grandson of Pequot Sachem, Sassacus

UNCAS, POMPI - b. ca. 1719, s. Benjamin and Ann Ceasar Uncas

UNCAS, SAM - b. ca. 1713, s. John Uncas; grandson of Uncas, Great Sachem of Mohegan Tribe; great grandson of Sassacus, Great Pequot Sachem; Norwich, Ct.

VANDERHOOP, ANNA E. - b. 1847, Feb.12, Gay Head, Ma. d. Wm. A. and Beulah Salsbury

VANDERHOOP, CUMMINGS B. - b. 1853, March 15, Gay Head, Ma., s. Wm. A. and Beulah Salsbury

VANDERHOOP, EDWIN - b. 1848, Dec. 12, Gay Head, Ma., s. Wm. A. and Beulah Salsbury

VANDERHOOP, JOHN PROSPERE - b. 1845, Mar. 26, Gay Head, Ma.

VANDERHOOP, LEONARD L. - b. 1855, Feb. 20, Gay Head, Ma.

VANDERHOOP, LOUISA E. - b. ca. 1840, d. Beulah and William A. Vanderhoop, Gay Head, Ma.

VANDERHOOP, NANNETTA - b. 1850, Jan. 4, Gay Head, Ma., d. Wm.A. and Beulah Salsbury

VANDERHOOP, PAULINA A. - b. 1843, May 15, New Bedford, Ma.,d. Wm.A. and Beulah Salsbury

VANDERHOOP, WM. ANDRIAAN - b. 1816, Jan.8, Parimaribo, Surinam, s. Frs. F. S. C. Vanderhoop of Holland

WAGHINACUT - b. s. Sowheag, Sachem of Wongunk, Middletown, Ct.

WAINER, ALBERT - b. ca. 1848, s. Mary Jane and Jeremiah Wainer, Dartmouth/Fall River Tribes; res., Westport, Ma.

BIRTHS

WAINER, ALEXANDER S. - b. ca. 1856, s. Mary J. and Asa F. Wainer, Dartmouth Tribe; res., Westport, Ma.

WAINER, AMELIA J. - b. ca. 1843, d. Mary J. and Asa F. Wainer, Dartmouth Tribe; res., Westport, Ma.

WAINER, ANN C. - b. ca. 1848, d. Mary J. and Asa F. Wainer, Dartmouth Tribe; res., Westport, Ma.

WAINER, CHARLES S. - b. ca. 1860, s. Lydia Ann and David E. Wainer, Dartmouth Tribe

WAINER, CHLOE D. - b. ca. 1847, d. Mary J. and Asa F. Wainer, Dartmouth Tribe; res., Westport, Ma.

WAINER, ELIZA K. - b. ca. 1841, d. Mary Jane and Jeremiah Wainer, Dartmouth/Fall River; res., Westport, Ma.

WAINER, EMELINE F. - b. ca. 1858, d. Mary J. and Asa F. Wainer, Dartmouth; res., Westport, Ma.

WAINER, FREDERICK D. - b. ca. 1855, s. David F.and Lydia Ann Wainer, Dartmouth Tribe

WAINER, GEORGE T. - b. ca. 1854, s. David F. and Lydia Ann Wainer, Dartmouth Tribe

WAINER, LOUISA - b. ca. 1854, d. Mary Jane and Jeremiah Wainer, Dartmouth Tribe; res.,Westport, Ma.

WAINER, LUCY L.S. - b. ca. 1858, d. Lydia Ann and David F. Wainer, Dartmouth Tribe

WAINER, MARIA E. - b. ca. 1860, d. Mary J. and Asa F. Wainer, Dartmouth Tribe; res., Westport, Ma.

WAINER, PAUL F. - b. ca. 1845, d. Mary Jane and Asa F. Wainer, Dartmouth Tribe; res.,Westport, Ma.

WAMPY, CLARINDA - b. 1791, d. Elijah and Elizabeth (Peters) Wampy

WAMPY, ELIJAH - b. 1734, Tunxis Tribe, Farmington, Ct.

WAMPY, ELIJAH - b. 1765, s. Elijah Wampy; res., lot 15, Brothertown, NY

WAMSLEY, AMEY - b. d. 1846, d. Eleanor and Hebron Wamsley, Gay Head Tribe; res., Gay Head, Ma.

WAMSLEY, BATHSHEBA - b. d. Paul and Phoebe (Jeffries) Wamsley

WAMSLEY, BENJAMIN - b. 1773, s. Paul and Phoebe (Jeffries) Wamsley

WAMSLEY, CELESTINE - b. ca. 1842, d. Eleanor and Hebron Wamsley, Gay Head Tribe; res., Gay Head, Ma.

BIRTHS

WAMSLEY, EPHRAIM - b. d. Paul and Phoebe (Jeffries) Wamsley

WAMSLEY, HARRIET A. - b. 1821, Sept.7, Gay Head, Ma., d. Salsbury Wamsley of Rochester, Ma. and Jane Robbins of Mashpee, Ma.

WAMSLEY, HEBRON - b. 1818, Jan. 17, Middleboro, Ma., s. Salsbury Wamsley of Rochester and Jane Robbins of Mashpee, Ma

WAMSLEY, HEBRON, Jr. - b. 1849, March 31, Gay Head, Ma., s. Hebron and Eleanor (Peters) Wamsley

WAMSLEY, JANE - b. 1771, d. Paul and Phebe (Jeffries) Wamsley

WAMSLEY, LAVINA H. - b. 1847, Feb. 6, Gay Head, Ma., d. Hebron and Eleanor (Peters) Wamsley

WAMSLEY, LYDIA - b. d. Paul and Phoebe (Jeffries) Wamsley

WAMSLEY, MARY - b. d. Paul and Phoebe (Jeffries) Wamsley

WAMSLEY, PAUL - b. s. Wamsley & Lydia Tuspaquin

WAMSLEY, PHOEBE - b. 1770, Feb. 26, d. Lydia Tuspaquin and Wamsley

WAMSLEY, PRISCILLA R. - b. 1865, Dec. 22, Gay Head, M., d. Hebron and Eleanor (Peters) Wamsley

WAMSLEY, TOLMAN - b. ca. 1843, s. Eleanor and Hebron Walmsley, Gay Head Tribe; res., Gay Head, Ma.

WAMSLEY, VALENTINE - b. 1857, Aug. 22, Gay Head, Ma., s. Hebron and Eleanor (Peters) Wamsley

WAMSLEY, WEALTHY - b. d. Paul and Phoebe (Jeffries) Wamsley

WAMSLEY, ZERVIAH - b. 176?, d. Wamsley & Lydia Tuspaquin

WANALANCET - b. s. Passaconaway

WAT - b. s. Isaac Nickanoose (Cheshechaamog); res., Podpis Village, Nantucket,Ma.; grandson of Wauwinet (Pomhaman); great grandson of Nickanoose; Nantucket, Ma.

WATSON, ALBERT - b. ca. 1815, R.I.; res., Stonington, Ct.

WATSON, AMY A. - b. ca. 1867 d. Rosella S. Watson of Narragansett Pier, R.I.

BIRTHS

WATSON, CHARLES - b. ca. 1868, s. Giles Watson; grandson of Thomas A. Watson

WATSON, EDWARD - b. ca. 1869, s. Rosella S. Watson of Narragansett Pier, R.I.

WATSON, EMMA - b. ca. 1841, Salem, Ct., d. Thomas A. Watson; res., Norwich, Ct.

WATSON, ESTHER - b. ca. 1819, South Kingstown, R.I.

WATSON, GILES - b. ca. 1843, Salem, Ct.; s. Thomas A. Watson; res., Rocky Hill, Ct.

WATSON, HANNAH B. - b. ca. 1859, Charlestown,R.I., d. of Charlotte (Conway)Watson

WATSON, ROSELLA S. - b. ca. 1837, Providence, R.I.; res., Narragansett Pier

WATSON, SARAH E. - b. ca. 1839, Salem,Ct.; d. Thomas A. Watson; res., Norwich

WATTAQUATINUSK (SARAH) - b. d. Wenepoykin (Sagamore George) and Ahawayetsquaine; granddaughter of Nanepashemet & Squaw Sachem; Salem, Ma.

WAUBY, ISAAC - b. 1762, s. Roger and Mary Wauby; res., lot 28, Brothertown, NY

WAUBY, JEHOIAKIM - b. 1791, s. Isaac and Jane (Patchauker) Wauby; res., lot 3, Brothertown, NY

WAUBY, JOSEPH - b. 1776, s. Roger and Mary Wauby; res., lot 33

WAUBY, ROGER - b. 1734; res., lot 3, Brothertown, NY

WAUCUS, JAMES - b. 1728, Tunxis Tribe, Farmington, Ct., s. James Wowowous, Tunxis Chief

WAUCUS, JAMES - b. 1768, s. James and Rachel Wowous; grandson of Farmington Chief

WAUCUS, MARY - b. 1793, d. James and Anne Curricomb Wiggins Titus; res., Brothertown, NY, lots 122, 123

WAUCUS, SAMSON - b. 1796. s. James and Anne (Curricomb) Wiggins Titus; res., lot 143, Brothertown, NY

WAUCUS, SUSANNAH - b. d. James and Rachel Wowous, Tunxis Tribe; Farmington, Ct.

WAUWINET - b. s. Nickanoose (Pomhaman)

WAUWOMPUHQUE, ABLE - b. s. Abel Wauwompuhque; grandson to Noatoasaet

BIRTHS

WAWARME - b. d. Sowheag, Chief of Wongunk Tribe, Middletown, Ct.; granddaughter of Saweag; great granddaughter of Sawash and wife Wawanda;

WEBQUISH, ESTELLA B. - b. ca. 1857, d. Jesse and Prudence P. Webquish, Mashpee Tribe; res., Mashpee, Ma.

WEBQUISH, FERDINAND - b. ca. 1858, s. William and Minerva, Mashpee Tribe; res., Mashpee, Ma.

WEBQUISH, JESSE - b. ca. 1828, s. Jesse and Prudence P. Webquish, Mashpee Tribe; res., New Bedford, Ma.

WEBQUISH, LEVI - b. ca. 1853, s. Levi S. and Anna F. Webquish, Mashpee Tribe; res., Mashpee, Ma.

WEEDEN, ALICE - b. ca. 1870, d. Louisa of Narragansett Pier, R.I.

WEEDEN, BERTHA - b. ca. 1865, d. Louisa Weeden of Narragansett Pier, R.I.

WEEDEN, GEORGE E. - b. May 12, 1880, s. Ida Weeden, South Kingstown, R.I.

WEEDEN, IDA - b. ca. 1854, South Kingston; res., South Kingstown, R.I.

WEEDEN, LOUISA - b. ca. 1844, Ct.; Narragansett Pier

WEEDEN, SARAH - b. ca. 1862, North Kingstown, R.I.; d. Charles & Eunice Weeden; res., North Kingstown, R.I.

WEEGRAMMOMENET - b. s. Tasunsquaw; grandson of Tahattawan,Nashoba Sachem (Thomas Waban) and Christian Indian; Concord, Ma

WEEKS, ELIZABETH - b.1 846, Feb. 28, Gay Head, Ma. d. Tristram and Tamson (Bunker) Weeks

WEEKS, TRISTRAM, Jr. - b. 1850, Aug.28, Gay Head, Ma., s. Tristram and Tamson (Bunker) Weeks

WENEPOYKIN - b. 1613, s. Nanampashemet & Squaw Sachem; res,. Salem, Ma.

WENUCHUS - b. d. Passaconaway of Penacook, NH

WESACHIPPAU, JEREMIAH - b. ca. 1687, s. Elisha Wesachippau and wife of Gay Head, Ma.

WHEELER, CHARLES H. - b. 1858, North Stonington, s. Eunice Wheeler of North Stonington

WHEELER, ELLA C. - b. ca. 1878, d. Josephine Wheeler of North Stonington

BIRTHS

WHEELER, JOSEPHINE - b. ca. 1841, Massachusetts, d. of Priscilla; res., North Stonington

WHEELER, PHEBE ANN - b. ca. 1874, d. Josephine Wheeler of North Stonington

WHEELER, SARAH PRISCILLA - b. ca. 1874, d. Josephine Wheeler of North Stonington

WHITING, ISABELLA F. - b. ca. 1838, d. Jane A. Whiting, Mashpee Tribe; res., Mashpee, Ma.

WHITING, LAURETTA L. - b. ca. 1844, d. Jane A. Whiting, Mashpee Tribe; res., Mashpee, Ma.

WHITTEN, HEPZIBAH - b. d. John & Jerusha Whitten

WIGGINS, MARTIN - b. 1791, s. James and Anne (Currecomb) Wiggins, Brothertown, NY

WIGGINS, MARY - b. 1793, d. James and Anne (Currecomb) Wiggins Titus; res., Brothertown, NY lots 122, 123

WIGGINS, SAMSON - b. 1796, s. James and Anne (Currecomb) Wiggins Titus; res., lot 143, Brothertown, NY

WILCOX, AMY A. - b. ca. 1872, d. Amy A. and O.S. Wilcox; res., South Kingstown, R.I.

WILCOX, IDA - b. ca. 1872, d. Amy A. and O.S. Wilcox; res., South Kingstown, R.I.

WILCOX, PATIENCE M. - b. ca. 1880, d. Amy A. and O. S. Wilcox; res., South Kingstown, R.I.

WILLIAMS, ADA E. - b. d. Lois Williams of Newport, R.I.

WILLIAMS, AMY - b. ca. 1878, grandchild of Harriet (Gardner) Simons of Westerly, R.I.

WILLIAMS, DANIEL H. - b. ca. 1876, s. Sarah F. (Harry) Williams of South Kingstown, R.I.

WILLIAMS, ELIZA - b. ca. 1815, d. Thomas Robinson; res., Prov., R.I.

WILLIAMS, GEORGE L. - b. ca. 1825; grandson of Thomas Robinson

WILLIAMS, JOHN - b. ca. 1879, grandson of Harriet Gardner Simons of Westerly, R.I.

WILLIAMS, LEWIS S. - b. ca. 1868, s. Sarah F. Harry Williams, grandson of Daniel and Mary Harry

WILLIAMS, LOIS E. - b. ca. 1836, Griswold, Ct.; res., Newport, R.I.

BIRTHS

WILLIAMS, NANCY - b. ca. 1831, Hopkinton, R.I., d.
Hannah (Babcock) & George L. Williams; res., New
London, Ct.

WILLIAMS, SARAH F. (HARRY) - b. ca. 1853, South
Kingstown, R.I.; d. Daniel & Mary Harry

WIOT, ROMANCE - b. 1826, s. Daniel and Rachel
Wiot of lot 88, Brothertown, NY

WIOT, THOMAS - b. ca. 1771; res., lot 135, Brothertown,
NY

WOIMPEGUAND - b. s. Musquntdowas and wife
Meekenump; grandson of Tamaquashad, Ancient Pequot
Sachem; Ct.

WOIMPEGUAND - b. s. Musquntdowas & Meekenump

WOIMPIGWOOIT - b. s. Woimpeguand and d. of
Narragansett Chief; grandson of Musquntdowas; great
grandson of Tamaquashad, Ancient Pequot Sachem; Ct.

WOMPANUMOO, MARTHA - b. d. Gershom & Sarah
Wompanummoo

WONOHAQUAHAM (SAGAMORE JOHN)- b. s. Nanepashemet,
Grand Sachem of Massachusetts Tribe; Lynn, Ma.

WOOD, SAMUEL - b. s. Abigail and Samuel Wood,
Herring Pond Tribe; res., Herring Pond

WUTTANOH, SAMUEL - b. s. Monataqua; grandson
of Wenepoykin and wife Ahawayetsquaine; great
grandson of Nanepashemet

WUTTONTAEHTUNNOCH, KATHERINE - b. d. of
Mechim & Suiokuman

MARRIAGES

MARRIAGES

AARON, JOSEPH - and Deborah, Grafton, Ma.;

AARON TOKOWASH, JOSEPH - and Sarah Muckamug, d. Sarah and Peter Muckamug, ca. 1737, Cumberland,

ABNER, HANNAH ABIGAIL - d. James & Mary Abner, and Thomas Commuck

ABNER, JAMES - s. Abner, of Pequot Tribe, Stonington, Ct., and Mary; res., Lantern Hill, Stonington, Ct.

ABNER, LUCY - d. Randall & Sarah (Tocus) Abner, and Stowe; second marriage to Coffin; Pequot Tribe, Stonington, Ct.

ABNER, MARIETTA - d. Randall & Sarah (Tocus) Abner, and John Welch; Pequot Tribe, Stonington, Ct.

ABNER, RANDALL - s. James & Mary Abner, and Sarah Tocus; Pequot Tribe, Stonington, Ct.; res., Kansas

ABNER, REBECCA - d. Randall & Sarah (Tocus) Abner, and Simeon Adams; second marriage to John W. Johnson; Pequot Tribe, Stonington, Ct.

ABNER, SILVIA - d. Randall & Sarah (Tocus) Abner, and Daniel Skeesuck; Pequot Tribe, Stonington, Ct.

ABEL, ABEGELL - and Israel Amos, Jan.27, 1757, Gay Head Congregational Church, Gay Head, Ma., by Rev. Zachary Hossueit Gay Head, Ma., Rev. Z. Hossueit

ABIMELECK, DAVID - of Hassanamisco Tribe, and sister to Andrew Abraham

ABIMELECK, ESTHER - d. Abimeleck, and Eliphalet Jowon, Mohegan Tribe, Montville, Ct.

ABRAHAM, ABEGAIL - and William Anthony, Nov. 14, 1752, Grafton, Ma.

ABRAHAM, ABIGAIL - d. Amy Printer of Hassanamisco Tribe, widow of Andrew, and Joseph Anthony

ABRAHAM, ANDREW - of Hassanamisco Tribe, and Abigail Printer, Feb. 29, 1739, Grafton, Ma.; married by Solomon Prentice

ACCOMES, HANNAH - and Benjamin Essil, Mar. 25, 1769, Gay Head Congregational Church, Gay Head, Ma., Rev. Zachary Hossueit

ACCOMES, THOMAS - and Hannah Skestomp, 1769, Gay Head Congregational Church, Gay Head, Ma., Rev. Zacharay Hossueit

79

MARRIAGES

ADAMS, DAMARIS - d. Solomon & Olive Occom, and Jacob Thomas; Tunxis Tribe, Farmington, Ct.; res., Farmington, Ct.

ADAMS, EDWIN C. - (Edwin Edwards Edwin Hathaway) and Lovina Matthews; Tunxis Tribe, and Lovina

ADAMS, EMELINE - d. Samuel & Mary (Fowler) Adams, and Lothrup Dick, res; Brothertown, Wisconsin

ADAMS, EMELINE - d. Samuel & Mary (Fowler) Adams, and Lothrup Dick

ADAMS, HANNAH - d. Samuel & Mary (Fowler) Adams, and Solomon Paul; Tunxis Tribe, Farmington, Ct.

ADAMS, JOHN - s. Adam, Tunxis Tribe, Farmington, Ct., of New Haven, Ct. and Sarah, 1756; res., Farmington, Ct.

ADAMS, JOHN - s. John & Sarah Adams of Brothertown, and Sarah Davies, b. 1748, widowed; res., Brothertown, NY, lot 6

ADAMS, JOHN - s. Samuel & Mary (Fowler) Adams, and Sally; res., Wisconsin, lot 126, Brothertown, NY

ADAMS, PHILENA - d. Solomon & Olive(Occom) Adams and James Waucus; second marriage to Thomas Crosley Tunxis Tribe, Farmington, Ct.; res., lots 96, 97, Brothertown

ADAMS, SAMUEL - s. Jacob, Quinnipiac Sachem, and Hannah Squamp,Wangunk Tribe, Ct; res., Brothertown.

ADAMS, SAMUEL - s. John, and Mary Fowler, d. of David Fowler; res., Brothertown, NY

ADAMS, SARAH - d. John & Sarah Adams, and Abraham Simons of Charleston, R.I.

ADAMS, SIMEON- s. Samuel & Mary (Fowler)Adams, and Rebecca Abner; res., Wisconsin

ADAMS, SOLOMON - s. Samuel & Hannah (Squamp) Adams, and Olive Occum d. of Rev. Samuel Occum; res., lot 52, Farmington, Ct.; emg. to eastern NY

ADAMS, THANKFUL - d. Samuel & Mary (Fowler) Adams, and Stevens; Tunxis Tribe, Farmington, Ct.

AEPJEN (WOIMPEGUAND) - s. Musguntdowas, grandson of Pequot Grand Sachem, Tamaquashad, and d. Narragansett Chief

MARRIAGES

AHANANIN, SARAH - and Jones, Paul

AHAWAYETSQUAINE (JOAN) - and Wenepoykin, Sachem and s. Namampashamet

AHHUNNUT, DINAH - d. Praying Indian, Panupuhquah, of Monument on the main land of Ma., and Henry Ahhunnut (Jannohquissoo)

AHHUNNUT, HANNAH (Pahkehtau) - of Martha's Vineyard and John Momonequem, s. Momonequem

AHHUNNUT, HANNAH (Pahkehtau) - of Martha's Vineyard, Ma. and Job Ahhunnut

AKOOCHIK, JOHNATHAN - and Jeruesha Ponue, Dec. 6, 1754, Gay Head Congregational Church, Rev. Zachary Hosueit

AKOOCHIK, MARCY - and Simon Papeneau, Nov. 13, 1750, Gay Head Congregational Church, Gay Head, Ma., Rev. Zachary Hossueit

AKOOCHIK, MARY - and Mathew Togoosin, June 25, 1767, Gay Head Congregational Church, Gay Head, Ma. Rev. Zachary Hossueit

AKKOMPOIN (WUTASAKOMPAUIN, JAMES PHILIP) - brother to Chief Massasoit,Wampanoag and Mary Neepanum of Pomposetticut Grand Sachem, and Mary Neepanum of Pomposetticut (Stow)

ALANOHCHANNUM - and John Tackanash; res., Nunpaug; in Edgartown, Ma.

ALVIS, JEMIMUK - and Joseph Quippish, Mashpee Indians

AMMAPOO (ABIGAIL) - d. Holmes Hole Sachem, Cheshchaamog and Wunnannanhkomun

AMMONS, AMOS - of Little Compton, R.I., and Rebecca Hinely of Dartmouth, Ma., March 8, 1764

AMOS, ABIAH - d. of Jonathan & Rachel Amos, and Elisha Paaonit

AMOS, HENRY - and Jude Gashim, Jan. 1, 1756, Gay Head Congregational Church, Gay Head, Ma., Rev. Zachary Hossueit

AMOS, ISRAEL - and Abegell Abell

AMOS, MARY - married Eleah Coshomon, Chilmark, Ma.

AMOS, REBECCA - and Hammond Watson, Mashpee Indians

MARRIAGES

AMOS, THOMAS - of Freetown and Elizabeth Ward int. Nov. 25, 1758

AMOS, THOMAS - of Freetown and Patience Ginnins of Westport, Jan. 2, 1789

ANTONE, ABIGAIL - and Joseph

ANTONE(Y), ABIGAIL - and Fortain Burn, Jan. 27, 1757, Grafton, Ma.; married by Charles Brigham, Justice of Peace

ANTHONY, ABRAHAM - of Dartmouth and Juda Case of Dartmouth, Ma. on Jan. 3, 1788 in Dartmouth, Ma.

ANTHONY, CHARLES - of Narragansett Tribe, and Lorinda Brushell; res., Wisconsin

ANTHONY, JOHN - married 1750, Sept. 6, Charlestown, RI, Sarah Ninigret (Sarah George), widow of George Ninigret, Sachem

ANTHONY, JOHN - and Betsey Mingo, Christiantown, Ma.; second marriage to Mary Cooper of Gay Head, Ma.

ANTHONY, JOSEPH - and Abigail Abram, Hassanamisco Indians

ANTHONY, MARY - married Frederick A. Lawton, Aug. 31, 1848, New Bedford, Ma.

ANTHONY, RACHEL - d. John & Betsey (Mingo) Anthoney, 1866, Jan. 16 and John H. Luley of Luley, Sandwich Island

ANTHONY, JOSEPH - married Abigail Antone, d. Ami Printer, ca. 1752, Grafton, Ma.

ANTHONY, JOSEPH - married Sally Auker, Dec. 2, 1821, Dartmouth, Ma.

ANTHONY, WILLIAM - married Abigail Abraham, Nov. 14, 1752, Grafton, Ma., married by Charles Brigham, Justice of Peace

ASKOMMOPOO - married Daniel Spotsor, (Wunannauhkomun)

ASSANNOOSHQUE - married James Cowkeeper

ASSWETOUGH - married Felix, Mashpee Tribe

ATTAWANHOOD - (Joshua), grandson of Sassacus, s. of Uncas, and Sougonusk, granddaughter of Rewen, d. Arramamet

ATTOMON, EXPERIENCE - d. Richard Attomon of Chaquesett Neck, and Moses Cussen 1730, Aug. 6;

MARRIAGES

ATTOMON, HOSEA - d. Richard Attomon of
Chaquesett Neck, and John Ralph

ATTOMON, RICHARD - of Chaquesett Neck, s. of
Attomonchassuck, Potonumecot Tribe, and Hester

ATTOMON, RICHARD - s. Richard & Hester Attomon,
and Betty Nopie, Aug. 6, 1730, second marriage to
daughter of Leah Cowley

ATTOMONCHASSUCK, SARAH - and Pepas Frances

AUCHOOUCH, HEPHZIBAH - and Jonathan Slocum
of Dartmouth, Ma., Dec. 6, 1772

AUKER, AMY P. - and Hebron Wamsley, April, 1809
(int.), Chilmark, Ma.

AUKER, BETSEY and Peleg Johnson, Nov. 23, 1823,
Dartmouth

AUKER, HANNAH TILLINGHAST - (SURNAME ALSO
WRITTEN PETIENT AND TITICUT) and Henry Cooper,
both of Freetown, Ma., Jan. 20 (23), 1753

AUKER, LURANA - and John Howell married
Dec. 29, 1805, New Bedford, Mass.

AUKER, ROBE of Dartmouth and Micael Wainer
of Westport, int. Dec. 2, 1814

AUKER, SALLY - of Westport, and Joseph Anthony,
of New Bedford, married Dec. 2, 1821, Dartmouth,
Ma. of Westport, and Cynthia Slocum, of New
Bedford, Ma., married June 29, 1830

AUKER, TILLINGHAST - of Wesport, and Cynthia
Slocum of New Bedford, Ma., married Dec. 2, 1821,
Dartmouth, Ma.

AWASHONKS - and Tolony, Little Compton, R.I. and
Waweyewett, Little Compton, R.I.

BACCHUS, TOBIAS WORNTON - slave of Capt.
Sargeant Winthrop, and Wampanoag Indian
woman, a domestic in family of Parsons

BAKEMAN, JOSIAH - and Helen, of Dudley Tribe:

BARKER, ISAAC - of Middleborough, Ma. and
Zurvia Carter, int. Mar. 17, 1760

BARKER, ISAAC - and Sarah Mun, Oct. 14, 1782,
Middleboro, Ma.

MARRIAGES

BARRAPAS, ISAAC - and Battey Cheeks, June 25,
1767, Gay Head Congregational Church, Gay Head,
Rev. Zachary Hossueit

BARTLETT, SOLOMON - of Herring Pond Tribe,
and oldest d. of Jonathan Lindsey

BARTLETT, SOLOMON - of Herring Pond Tribe and
Betsey Lindsey, d. of Jonathan Lindsey:

BASSET, JULIA - and Samuel Smalley of New York,
m. 1860, Jan. 22

BASSET, LEANDER - and Huldah Jeffers, July 25, 1832

BEARSE, JOSEPH - and Martha Taylor of Yarmouth, Ma.

BEARSE, JOSIAH - and Mary Sissel of Watuppa
Reservation, 1718

BELAIN, GEORGE J. - and Sophia Peters, 1836

BELAIN, MELISSA - and James W. Jeffers, and Levi Cuff

BERRY, RHODA - and Thomas Buchanan

BOWMAN, ELISHA - and Aaron Whipple (Joseph)

BOWYER, JAMES - and Olive B. Francis, 1864,
Dec. 1

BROOKS, THOMAS - and Nancy Nickerson (white);
res., Dennis, Ma. area:

BRUSHEL, HENRY - s. Samuel Brushel, and Nancy
Welch Brushel, widow of brother Samuel; Mohegan
Tribe, Mohegan, Ct.; emg. to Wisconsin

BRUSHEL, LORINDA - d. Sampson & Betsey (Ceipet)
Brushel and Charles Anthony, of Narragansett Tribe,
Charlestown, R.I.; emg. to Wisconsin, 1837

BRUSHEL, LUCINDA - d. Samuel Brushel, and Welch;
res., emg. from Mohegan, Ct. to Wisconsin

BRUSHEL, LYDIA - d. Samuel Brushel, and Aaron
Toucee, Mohegan Tribe, Mohegan, Ct.

BRUSHEL, NANCY - d. Samuel Brushel, and Hart,
of Pequot Tribe, Stonington, Ct.; res., Brothertown

BRUSHEL, SAMPSON - s. Abigail Brushel, and
Betsey Ceipet; res., lots 127 & 34, Brothertown

BRUSHEL, SAMUEL - s. Abigail, and Esther; second
marriage to Abigail Skeesuch; Mohegan Tribe,
Mohegan, Ct.

MARRIAGES

BRUSHEL, SAMUEL - s. Samuel Brushel, and Nancy
Welch, Mohegan Tribe, Mohegan, Ct.

BRUSHEL, THOMAS - s. Samuel and Hannah Cujep;
Mohegan Tribe, Mohegan , Ct., res., Brothertown

BUCHANAN, MARY - and Chapman

BUNKER, TAMSON - and William Thomas, ca. 1841,
Gay Head, Ma.

BURNEE, FORTUNE - and Abigail Printer, d. Sarah Printer,
Grafton, Ma.

BURNEE, FORTUNE - and Phylis of Mendon, Ma.,
July 31,1778, in Grafton, Ma. by Daniel Grosvenor,
Pastor; 1778

BURNEE, FORTUNE - and Sarah Robbins of
Hassanamisco Tribe, ca. 1750

BURNEE, FORTUNE - of Grafton, Ma. and Sarah
Hector of Sutton, Ma., in Grafton, Nov. 8, 1781, by
Daniel Grosvenor, Pastor

BURNEE, SARAH - of Grafton, Ma. and Boston Philips
of Grafton, Ma., in Grafton, Ma., married, July 9, 1786,
by Benjamin Goddard, Justice of Peace

BURNEE, SARAH - of Grafton, and Prince Dom of
Woodstock, April 20, 1771, Smithfield, Ma.

CAHKUHQUIT, SARAH - d. Samson & Elizabeth
Cahkuhquit, and Jacob Peag

CAIN, JEMIMA - and James Shaa

CAKENAHEW, JUDA - and Ceasor, Oct. 14, 1765,
Dartmouth, Ma.

CANONICUS (Meika,Mexanno) - and Matantuck
(Quiapen, Magnus, Sunksquaw, Old Queen),
sister to Ninigret

CARRIER, CORNELIA - and Francis Hemmenway,
Mar. 9, 1841, Middleboro, Ma.

CARTER, AMIE - of Swanze and Gideon Woodmansee
of Dartmouth, Oct. 7, 1781

CARTER, ZURVIA - of Dartmouth, int. to marry Isaac
Barker of Middleboro, March 17, 1760

CAUTE, LEDEH - and Johnathan Elisha, Oct. 11, 1750,
Gay Head, Congregational Church, Gay Head, Ma.,

MARRIAGES

Rev. Zachary Hossueit

CEASAR, ANN - d. Ceasar, Sachem of Mohegans from 1715-1723 and Ben Poquiom, son of Major Ben Poquiom

CEASAR, LUCY - and Ezekine Alvis, Mashpee Indians

CEASAR, MOSES - of Hassanamisco Tribe, m. Laney Jefferson,

CEIPET, BENJAMIN - and Hannah, res.; Brothertown, lot 35

CHARLES, - and Rhoda Niles, d. of James Niles of Narraganset Tribe

CHARLES, EUNICE - d. of Josiah & Jerusha Peters, and David Toucee; second marriage to William Crosley; res.; Brothertown

CHARLES, GEORGE - of Stonington and Sarah Obediah of Dartmouth, int. Sept. 1774

CHARLES, JOSIAH - and Jerusha Peters, d. George Peters; res., Brothertown, lot 102

CHARLES, RHODA, - widow of Charles, and Daniel Wauby

CHACE, ALICE, - d. Joseph Chace, and Cato Northrup; res. Providence; Troy Indians

CHASE, REUBEN - a Dennis, Ma. resident, and Polly, Yarmouth Indian

CHASE, REUBEN, Jr. - s. Reuben and Polly Chase, and Nancy; res., Yarmouth, Ma.

CHAUGHM, (QUAM), JAMES - and Molly Barber, res., Barkhamstead, Ct., Lighthouse Tribe

CHOKO, JAMES - and Diana Tossman, int. Sept. 26, 1730, Freetown, Ma.

CHURCH, MALLE - and Absolam Gardner, Mul., May/June 1732, Freetown, Ma.

COCHEAT, CHARLES - and Sophia Crosley; Pequot Tribe, Groton, Ct.; res., lot 82, Brothertown

COMMUCK, ALICE E. - d. Thomas & Hannah (Abner) Commuck, and Rhodolphus M. Fowler; res., Brothertown, Wisconsin

COMMUCK, ALZUMA - d. Thomas & Hannah (Abner) Commuck, and Toxuse, Brothertown, Wisconsin

MARRIAGES

COMMUCK, HELEN - d. Thomas & Hannah (Abner) Commuck & Frank LaBelle

COMMUCK, SARAH PRENTICE - d. Thomas & Hannah (Abner) Commuck, and Orville A. Hart

COMMUCK, THOMAS - s. Joseph Chummuck, and Hannah Abner, July 31, 1831; of Narragansett Tribe, Charlestown, RI; emg. to Brothertown, Wis., ca. 1831

CONET, CYNTHIA - d. John and Phebe Lindsey Conet, and Solomon Attaquin of Mashpee Tribe

CONET, JOHN - of Herring Pond Tribe and Phebe Lindsey, d. Jonathan Lindsey

COOK, JOSEPH - Tiverton, R.I. and Mary Prince, July 15, 1785, Dartmouth, Ma.

COMPSIT, DINAH - and Issachar Cato, free Negro, Jan. 3, 1771, int., Scituate, Ma.

CONQUANCE, - and Bettie Thomson, Indians of Bridgewater in Bridgewater, Ma. on May 29,1755

COOPER, AARON - of Gay Head, Ma., s. Abiah & Aaron Cooper, Lucy Peters, May 30, 1840

COOPER, AARON - and Phebe Pocknet, m. 1847, Sept.18

COOPER, ABIAH - and Aaron Cooper

COOPER, BIAH - of Chilmark, Ma., and John Cuff, Nov. 2, 1783, Dartmouth, Ma.

COOPER, BELINDA, of Gay Head, Ma., and Thomas Mores, 29, 1755

COOPER, ELIZABETH N. - and Wm. Jeffers, 1859, Apr. 16, Gay Head

COOPER, GEORGE W. - s. Thomas & Susannah Talknot Cooper, and Sarah Pocknet

COOPER, GEORGIANA E. - of Gay Head, d. Aaron & Phoebe Pocknet, and Sylvester Powell, 1869, 27th day

COOPER, LOUISA - of Gay Head, Ma., and George Davis, Sept. 17, 1836, Chilmark, Ma.

COOPER, LUCINA - d. Mary Cooper & Henry James, and Thomas Jeffers

COOPER, MARY - and Thomas Jeffers, 1755

COOPER, MARY and John A. Spencer

MARRIAGES

COOPER, MARY - b.1784, d. Mary (Harry) & Thomas Cooper, and Johnson Peters, b. Jan. 27, 1782, Chabbaquiddick, m. 1807, Oct.

COOPER, MARY - b.1814, d. Johnson & Mary (Cooper) Peters,and Henry James,1755

COOPER, THOMAS - s. Thomas & Susannah (Talknot) Cooper and Jane Wormseley, May 7, 1837

COOPER, THOMAS - and Susannah Talknot

COOPER, THOMAS - and Mary Lishas Henry Dec. 7, 1756, Gay Head Congregational Church, Gay Head, Ma., Rev. Zachary Hossueit

COOPER, ZACCHEUS - s. Thomas & Susannah (Talknot) and Martha Attaquin of Mashpee, Ma., 1848, Apr.6

CORY, JUPITER - a Mustee, and Eunice Crocker, a Mustee, of Dartmouth, Sept. 3, 1783

CORSEY, ABBY ANN - d. Julia F. (Jeffers) & London Corsey, and John Prospere Vanderhoop

COTTLE, ESTHER - d. Hester (Daggett) & Edward Cottle, and Harding of Tisbury, Ma.

COWKEEPER, JOSEPH - of Edgartown & Assanooshque (Old Sarah) who d. 1703, Edgartown

COYHIS (Coys, Cohoize, Coghooisze), BENJAMIN J.- s. John & Martha (Dick) Coyhis, and Laura; second marriage to Rosella S.; res., Wisconsin

COYHIS (Coys, Cohoize, Coghooisze), JOHN - s. William & Mary Coyhis, and Martha Dick, d. of Asa Dick; res., lot 52, Brothertown

COYHIS (Coys, Cohoize, Coghooisze), JOHN R. - s. John & Martha (Dick) Coyhis, and Sophia Sampson

COYHIS (Coys, Cohoize, Coghooisze), WILLIAM - s. Ephraim & Mary; Narragansett Tribe, Charlestown, RI; res., Brothertown

CRANK, CATHERINE - Fall River Indian, and Elisha Simpson

CROCKER, EUNICE - Mustee, of Dartmouth and Jupiter Cory, Mustee, of Dartmouth, Sept. 3, 1783

CROCKER, LOUISA - Penobscot Indian, and William Perry

CROSLEY, CAROLENE - d. William Crosley, and Daniel Jakeways

MARRIAGES

CROSLEY, ELIZABETH - d. George Crosley, and
John Hammer

CROSLEY, GEORGE - and Lornhamah; second marriage to
Elizabeth (Fowler) Scippio widow to Obadiah Scippio;
Pequot Tribe, Stonington, Ct.; res., Brothertown NY, Lot 2

CROSLEY, GRACE ANN - b. 1776, d. George of Pequot
Tribe, married Joseph Tocus of Charlestown, RI; res.,
lot 59, Brothertown, NY

CROSLEY, JOHN - s. William Crosley, and Parmelia
Fowler, d. Hesekiah Fowler

CROSLEY, KATHARINE - d. George, & William Dick

CROSLEY, LUCENETTE (LUREANETT) - d. Thomas
& Philena (Adams) Crosley, and Alonzo D. Dick

CROSLEY, LUCINA - and Thomas Jeffers

CROSLEY, SEREPTA - d. Wm. Crosley, and Elias
Jacob Dick, s. Elkahah & Sarah Ann (Toucee)Dick

CROSLEY, SOPHRONIA - d. Thomas & Philena
(Adams) Crosley, and Doxstater

CROSLEY, THOMAS - s. George Crosley, and
Philena, d. of Solomon & Olive Occum Crosley;
res., lots 76, 96, 97, Brothertown, NY

CROSLEY, WILLIAM - s. Philena (Adams) & Thomas
Crosley, and Hannah Dick, d. of William Dick; second
marriage to Aurilla Dick, d. of Thomas Dick; third
marriage to Eunice Charles, d. of Josias Charles

CUFF, SARAH (DEN) - of Westport, and Baston, a
Negro, of Freetown, int. Sept. 19,1788

CUJEP (CHUCHIP), PRUDENCE - d. Sampson &
Eunice Pouquenup, a widow, second marriage to
Gideon Harry; res., lot 104, Brothertown, NY

CURLISS, CHRISTOPHER - and Nancy Pollock,
daughter of Mingo Pollock and Dudley Indian Woman

CURLISS, MARY - d. Nancy (Pollock) and Christopher
Vickers

**CURRICOMB (CORCOM, CURRACOMP, CORRECOMPT,
ACCORRECOMPT), ANDREW** - s. Andrew, and Abigail;
Tunxis Tribe, Farmington, Ct.; res., lots 120, 121;
Brothertown, NY

MARRIAGES

CURRICOMB (CORCOM, CURRACOMP, CORRECOMPT, ACCORRECOMPT), **ANNE** - d. Andrew & Abigail Curricomb, and James Wiggins; res., lots 122, 123, Brothertown, NY

CURRICOMB (CORCOM, CURRACOMP, CORRECOMPT, ACCORRECOMPT), **ELIAKIM** - s. Andrew Curricomb, and Martha Onion; res., lots 57, 58, Brothertown, NY

CURRICOMB (CORCOM, CURRACOMP, CORRECOMPT, ACCORRECOMPT), **ELIZABETH** - d. Andrew Curricomb, and Benjamin Toucee; res., lot 20, Brothertown, NY

CURRICOMB (CORCOM, CURRACOMP, CORRECOMPT, ACCORRECOMPT), **JESSE** - s. Andrew Curricomb, and Phebe; res., Brothertown NY, lots 120, 121

DANIEL, PETER - of Plymouth, Ma., and Sarah Waterman of Plymouth int. Jan. 24,1733

DAVID, ALEXANDER - and Ann Judson, 1865, July 16; Gay Head, Ma.

DAVID, ELIZABETH - and Tip White, Dartmouth, Ma., Jan. 5, 176?

DAVID, PRUDENCE - and Alexander Nevers, 1870, Mar. 8; Gay Head, Ma.

DAVIES, HENRY - and Sarah; res., lot 6, Brothertown

DIAMOND, JAMES - and Abiah Manning,1857

DICK, ABIGAIL - d. William & Hannah (Potter) Dick, and David Johnson, res., Wis.

DICK, ALEXANDER - s. Paul, and Samantha Sekeeter, d. John Seketer; res., lot 81, Brothertown, NY; Wis. (1832); Kansas (1852)

DICK, ALONZO DAVID - s. Paul of Charleston, R.I., res., lot 129, Brothertown, NY, and Luranett Crosley, d. Dismiss Kuish; granddaughter of Philip Kuish; res.,

DICK, ELLEN JANE - and Oscar Johnson married 1867, Dec. 22

DICK, ELIZABETH d. William & Hannah (Potter) Dick, and Rhodolphus Fowler res., lot 113, Brothertown, NY

DICK, EUNICE - and James Wamby; res., Wis.

DICK, HANNAH - d. William & Hannah (Potter) Dick, and William Crosley; emg. to Wisconsin, 1834

MARRIAGES

DICK, HARRIET - and Joseph Scanandoa

DICK, JOSEPH - and Pashonis Tohqun, Nov. 1, 1754, Gay Head Congregational Church, Gay Head, Ma., Rev. Zachary Hossueit

DICK, LOTHRUP - s. William & Hannah (Potter) Dick, and Emeline Adams; res., 124, Brothertown; emg. to Wisconsin in 1834

DICK, LUCENA - d. William & Hannah (Potter) Dick, and George Sampson, res., lot 112, Brothertown, NY

DICK, LUCIUS C. - and Sarah

DICK, MARY and Frankford Slocum of Dartmouth, Ma., Nov. 15, 1760

DICK, PATIENCE - d. William & Hannah (Potter) and James Fowler; res., lot 100, Brothertown, NY

DICK, SOPHIA - d, Paul and Hannah (Fowler) Dick (Richards) and Peter Cooper, Oneida Indian

DICK, WILLIAM - and Hannah Potter; Narragansett Tribe, Charlestown, R.I.; res., lot 135, Brothertown, NY

DIVINE, PATRICK - and Louisa Pocknet, 1844, April 2; Gay Head, Ma.

DURFEE, CHARLES - and Mary Mingo

ELISHA, ABNER - and Polly Slocum, Dartmouth, Nov. 11,1784

EPHRAIM, DEBORAH - and Job Prince, int. Nov. 22, 1763, Dartmouth,Ma.

EPHRAIM, HANNAH - of Dartmouth and John Rady, of Dartmouth, Ma., May 23, 1765

EPHRAIM, HESTER - and David Butterfield, Negro, Jan. 5, 1765, Dartmouth, Ma.

ESSIL, BENJAMIN - and Hannah Accomes Mar. 25, 1769, Gay Head Congregational Church Gay Head, Ma., Rev. Zachary Hossueit

FELIX, ISRAEL - and Deliverance Cowit, Dec. 26, 1746, Barnstable

FELIX, ISRAEL - and Hope Paris in Middleboro,Ma.

FOWLER, ABBA LORETTA - Sept. 19, 1843 and Edgar Morris Dick, b. Oct. 28, 1843, Brothertown, Wis.

FOWLER, ABIGAIL - d. James Fowlerand Laton Dick, July 14,1797; res., lot 78, Brothertown, NY;

MARRIAGES

FOWLER, ALEXANDER - s. Jacob and Amy S. Potter and Desdemona Dick, d. Wm. Dick

FOWLER, ALEXANDER, s. Jacob and Amy S. Potter and Harriet Dick, d. Asa and Nancy Skeesuck, d. Daniel Skeesuck

FOWLER, BENJAMIN GARRETT - and Temperance Pharaoh of Brothertown, NY and Elizabeth Skeesuck, widow of Arnold Skeesuck, res., lot 62

FOWLER, DAVID - s. James, b. 1735, and Hannah Garrett, m. 1766, res., lot 105, lot 119, Brothertown, NY

FOWLER, DAVID - and Phebe Kiness, married 1791 res., lot 16

FOWLER, DAVID - and Elizabeth Simons, d. James Simons; res., Brothertown, Wis.

FOWLER, HANNAH - and Paul Dick , of Charlestown, R.I., Narragansett Tribe

FOWLER, HARRIET - Adelaide and John Niles, 1864, Nov. 24

FOWLER, HEZEKIAH - and Fanny F. Skeesuck

FOWLER, JACOB - and Amy Potter; res., lot 141, Brothertown, NY

FOWLER, JAMES - and Sarah Simmons; res., lot 103 (1817), lot 111 (1828), Brothertown, NY

FOWLER, JOHN - b. Sept. 19, 1817, Brothertown, NY and Phebe

FOWLER, NILES - d. James Niles; res., Wis.

FOWLER, LATON - s. James and Patience Dick, and Elizabeth Dick, d. Elkannah Dick

FOWLER, LORENZO DAVID - s. Jacob and Amy S. Potter, and Mary V. Johnson, d. Emanuel Johnson

FOWLER, LUCIUS SYRENIUS - b. May 10,1819. Brothertown, NY and Phebe Fowler res., Wis.

FOWLER, LURA, d. B. G. Fowler and Nelson Paul, s. Samson Paul of Brothertown, NY

FOWLER, MARY - and Samuel Adams, s. John Adams; res., Brothertown, NY

FOWLER, MARY - and Samson Occom

FOWLER, MARTHA - and Emanuel Johnson; res., lot 61, Brothertown, NY

MARRIAGES

FULLER, DAVID - and Hannah Williams, Ma.

FULLER, DAVID - and Nancy Freeman, Ma.

FULLER, DAVID - and Sylvia Prince, Ma.

GARDNER, ELIZA - d. Jane Lindsey and Roland T. Gardner of Herring Pond Tribe, and Mye, Ma.

GARDNER, ELIZABETH - d. Jane Lindsey and Roland T. Gardner of Herring Pond Tribe, and Ellis, barber at Sandwich, Ma.

GARDNER, EUNICE - d. Charlotte Potter, and Primos Wheeler

GARDNER, ISABELLA - d. Jane Lindsey and Roland T. Gardner of Herring Pond Tribe, and Nickerson

GARDNER, MARIA - d. Jane Lindsey and Roland T. Gardner of Herring Pond Tribe and Warren Fletcher

GARDNER, SALLY - d. Jane Lindsey and Roland T. Gardner of Herring Pond Tribe, and Ralph Blackwell of Herring Pond Tribe

GARDNER, WILLIAM - and Mary Tobey, d. of Joseph Tobey of Mashpee, Ma.

GASHIM, AARON - and Jemima Wossonon, Jan. 26, 1749/50, Gay Head Congregational Church, Gay Head, Ma., Rev. Zachary Hossueit

GASHIM, JUDE - and Henry Amos, Jan. 1,1756, Gay Head Congregational Church, Gay Head, Ma., Rev. Zachary Hossueit

GASHIM, MARTHA - and Joseph Ski....., Feb. 15, 1760, Gay Head Congregational Church, Gay Head, Ma., Rev. Zachary Hossueit

GASHIM, SARAH - and Benjamin Pito, Nov. 13, 1767, Gay Head Congregational Church, Gay Head, Ma., Rev. Zachary Hossueit

GEORGE, ABEL - and Jean Ham, Jan. 7, 1758, Gay Head Congregational Church, Gay Head, Ma., Rev. Zachary Hossueit

GIBBS, JOHN (AWAASAMOG) - and Hannah Joseph, Sept. 15, 1790

GIMBEE, CESAR of Hassanamisco Tribe, and Patence

GOULD, BETSEY and James Hill, Lakeville, Ma.

GOULD, JANE S. - and John Williams, Lakeville, Ma.

MARRIAGES

GOULD, LYDIA - and Antoniao D. Juliao, 1819,
Nov. 22; Lakeville, Ma.

GOULD, RUBY - and Benjamin Hall, Lakeville, Ma.

GOULD, ZERVIAH - and Thomas Mitchell, Lakeville, Ma.

HAM, JEAN - and George Abel

HAMMOND, BETTY - and Richard Gool, Dec. 3, 1762,
Middleboro, Ma.

HARDING, ABIAH - and Locke of Maine

HARDING, ANNA - and James Wyman of Belgrade, Maine

HARDING, EPHRAIM - and Rebucca Luce, 1809,
Aug. 26, Chilmark

HARDING, THOMAS - and Betsy Baxter,1808, Aug. 20

HARDING, WILLIAM - and Sarah E Norton,1844,
Feb. 26, Tisbury, Ma.

HARDING, SHUBAEL - and Abiah Luce, before 1744

HARRIS, LORA - and John Terry, April 29, 1808,
Middleboro, Ma.

HARRY, JEMIMAH - and Isaac Pemannunit, Feb. 13,
1756, Gay Head Congregational Church, Gay Head,
Ma., Rev. Zachary Hoosueit

HATHAWAY, JOSEPH - and Mercy Prince, of
Dartmouth, Aug. 25, 1773

HAZARD, PERRY G. - of Charlestown, R.I. and Caroline
Holmes, of Narragansett Tribe

HECTOR, MONDAY - of Hassanamisco Tribe and Lucy
C. Lawrence

HECTOR, JOHN of Hassanamisco Tribe and Jukey
Toney of Royalston, Ma.

HENDRICK, SOLOMON - and Catherine Quinney

HENRY, MARY LISHAS - and Thomas Cooper, Dec. 7,
1756, Gay Head Congregational Church, Gay Head,
Ma., Rev. Zachary Hoosueit

HILL, KEZIAH - and Camoralsman Gould

HOHPEN, ELIS - and Joseph Tallman, Dec. 30, 1768,
Gay Head Congregational Church, Gay Head, Ma.,
Rev. Zachary Hoosueit

HOSUIT, ANN - and Daniel Nevers of Gay Head, m.
1868, Jan. 16; Gay Head, Ma.

MARRIAGES

HOSSUEIT, ABEGAIL - and Samuel Pance Jr., Jan. 3, 1758, Gay Head Congregational Church, Gay Head, Ma.

HOSSUEIT, MARY - and Abill Setam, 29th day, Gay Head Congregational Church, Gay Head, Ma., Rev. Zachary Hoosueit

HOSSUEIT, SARAH - and John Ohkoh, Dec. 9, 1757, Gay Head Congregational Church, Gay Head, Ma., Rev. Zachary Hoosueit

HOSSUEIT, SUUSONOH - Abel George, Dec. 13, 1754, Gay Head Congregational Church, Gay Head, Ma., Rev. Zachary Hoosueit

HOSSUEIT, ZACHARY,Jr. - and Sarah Tallmon, Dec. 10, 1760, Gay Head Congregational Church, Gay Head, Ma., Rev. Zachary Hoosueit

HOWWASSWEE, OLIVE - and William Mingo

HOWWASSWEE, OLIVE - and Josiah Jerrett

HOWWASSWEE, ZACCHEUS - Elizabeth Wamsley

HYANO, JOHN - and Mary

HYANO, MARY - and Austin Bearse, 1639

JACKSON, JACOB - and Mary Bancroft; res., Bellingham, Ma.

JACOBS, MARY - and James Borden, Dartmouth, Ma.

JAMES, HENRY G. - and Mary Cooper Peters

JAMES, WILLIAM S. - and Avis Divine

JEFFERS, HULDAH - and Leander Bassett

JEFFERS, THOMAS - and Sarah, Sept, Aug. 25, 1782, Middleboro, Ma.

JEFFERY, BENJAMIN - of Plympton, Ma., and Thankful Barker, Dec. 25, 1783, Middleboro, Ma.

JEFFERY, LYDIA - of Dartmouth, Ma., and Samuel Gray

JEFFERY, LYDIA - of New Bedford, Ma., and Isaac N. Barker, Jan. 17, 1810

JEFFERY, LYDIA - and Charles H. Mingo, Nov. 21, 1861; Gay Head, Ma.

JEFFERY, PHEBE - and Paul Squin

JENNINGS, PEGE - and Pompe Peckcom of Dartmouth, Oct. 13, 1773

JOB, MARTHA - of Dartmouth, Ma., and Peter Quonnwin (Quonaawe) of Tiverton, R.I., May 23, 1763

MARRIAGES

JOEL, JOHN - and Mary Tallmon, May 8, 1758, Gay Head Congregational Church, Gay Head, Ma., Rev. Zachary Hossueit

JOEL, JUDE - and Silas Philip, Dec.14, 1753, Gay Head Congregational Church, Gay Head, Ma., Rev. Zachary Hossueit

JOEL, SIMON - and Jemimah Philip, May 8, 1758, Gay Head Congregational Church, Gay Head, Ma., Rev. Zachary Hossueit

JOHNSON, ABIGIAL - d. Wm. and Charlotte (Skeesuck) Johnson of Wis., and George Skeesuck

JOHNSON, ALEXANDER HOWARD - of New Bedford, Ma. and Mary Ann Vickers Johnson

JOHNSON, CALEB - of Dartmouth, Ma. and Mercy Terry, of Assonet, Ma., m. 1806

JOHNSON, COLLEN BARDT - s. John Johnson, and Electa Scipio

JOHNSON, DAVID - s. Emanuel and Martha Fowler, and Abigail Dick; res., Wis.

JOHNSON, ESTHER - d. William, and John Crosley Hammer, s. John Hammar

JOHNSON, EUNICE - d. Emanuel Johnson of lot 61, Brothertown, NY, and Nathan Crosley Dick

JOHNSON, HENRY - and Avis Sampson

JOHNSON, JAMES - and Zerviah Squin, Nov. 27, 1791

JOHNSON, JEREMIAH - s. Emanuel and Martha (Fowler), and Jemima Dick; res., Wis.

JOHNSON, JOHN W. - and Rebecca Abner, wid. Adams

JOHNSON, JOSEPH - s. Joseph Johnson, and Tabitha Occom, d. Rev. Samson Occom, m. Dec. 2, 1773

JOHNSON, JOSEPH - s. Joseph and Tabitha Johnson, and Sarah, 1799; res., Brothertown NY, lots 133, 134

JOHNSON, JULIA ANN - and Moses Pocknet, m. 1870, May 8; Gay Head, Ma.

JOHNSON, NANCY - d. Wm. and Charlotte (Skeesuck) Johnson, and Jonathan Schooner

JOHNSON, ORLANDO D. - and Almira J. Sampson

JOHNSON, ORRIN - s. William and Charlotte Skeesuck, and Wealthy J. Fowler

MARRIAGES

JOHNSON, ORRIN - s. William and Charlotte Skeesuck,
and Mary, d. Peter Crowell; res., Minnesota

JOHNSON, OSCAR - and Ellen Jane Dick, 1867,
Dec. 22; Wis.

JOHNSON, PETER - and Rachel Turner

JOHNSON, RICHARD - s. William and Hannah N.
(Perry) Johnson, and Alice Pequit,

JOHNSON, ROWLAND - and Almira Dick, 1840,
Nov. 18, and Barbara Dick

JOHNSON, SIMON - and Emily G. Cook

JOHNSON, WILLIAM and Sarah Cheevers Rooks, Jan. 1,
1849, New Bedford, Ma.

JOHNSON, WILLIAM - s. John Johnson of Brothertown,
NY, and Charlotte Skeesuck, d. John and Ann Skeesuck
of Charlestown, R.I., Narragansett Tribe

JOHNSON, WILLIAM HENRY - and Hannah Niles Perry,
d. Wm and Nancy (Niles) Smith of Charlestown, R.I.,
Middleboro, Ma., June 28, 1836, New Bedford, Ma.

JONAS, EDWARD - and Sil Sibit, Nov. 26, 1789
Middleboro, Ma.

JONES, HANNAH - and Prince Caswell, Nov. 24, 1779
Middleboro, Ma.

JONES, JOSEPH - of Tiverton, and Marcy Prince of
Dartmouth July 15, 1785

JONES, WILLIAM - Mashpee Tribe, and Antoinette Murray

JOSEPH, JABEZ - and Patience Oliver, Aug. 6, 1747,
Rochester

KINDNESS, JAMES - s. Thomas and Phebe Kindness
of lot 78, Brothertown, NY, and Hannah Dick

LAUTON (Lawton), LUCINDA - and Abraham Anthony

LAUTON (Lawton), JOHN - and Jane Squin, April 13, 1823,
Middleboro, Ma.

LAUTON (Lawton), LUCY CEASAR - and Monday
Hector, Hassanamisco Indians

LAUTON (Lawton), PETER - and Sarah Printer, d. Moses
Printer, Hassanamisco Indians

LAWRENCE, CEASAR - and Patience Printer,
Hassanamisco Indians

MARRIAGES

LAWRENCE, LUCY CEASAR - of Hassanamisco Tribe and Monday Hector

LAWTON, ABRAHAM - and Patience Toworey, of Dartmouth, Ma., Nov. 14, 1778, Lucinda Derry

LAWTON, ELIZABETH - of Freetown & Oliver Slade of Swan. May 6, 1784, by David Simmons

LEE, WILLIAM - (William Ewing) of Middleboro and Emeline Cowit: res., Lakeville, Ma.

LINDSEY, JANE - d. Jonathan Lindsey m. Roland T. Gardner, Herring Pond Tribe

LINDSEY, PHEBE - d. Jonathan Lindsey, m. John Conet of Herring Pond Tribe

MADISON, ANN JUDSON - and Samuel J. Haskins

MADISON, CHARLOTTE - and Samuel J. Haskins, 1868, Jan. 3

MADISON, MICHAEL - and Diana Peters, 1830, June 2, and Roxa Lowee

MANNING, ALVIN - and Roxa Lowee and Mary Kent, of Vt.

MANNING, LORANA - and Ebenezer Sisson, June 25, 1827, Middleboro, Ma.

MANNING, THOMAS - and Rosabella M. Howwassee

MANUEL, MARY - and William Thomas, Natick Indian

MATTHEWS, JOHN - s. Eliphalet Adams and Elizabeth (Crosley) Matthews, and Adelia Sampson, d. George Sampson; res., Wis.

MATTHEWS, RANSOM - s. Eliphalet Adams and Elizabeth (Crosley) Matthews, and Maria Sampson, d. George Sampson; res., Brothertown, Wis.

MEEKSISHQUNE - and Zachariah Osooit

METOXIN, JOHN - and daughter of Andrew & Jane Quinney Miller

MIANTONOMO - and Wawarme

MICHEL, JOHN E. - and Ada F. Noka, d. Joshua Noka; res., Richmond

MILLER, CEASAR - of African descent, and Mary Simmons, of Mohawk Tribe

MILLER, CHARLES - s. Mary Simmons and Ceasar Miller, and Lucretia

MARRIAGES

MILLER, MARY - Simmons, former spouse of Ceasar, a Mohawk Indian, and William Warner, in New Bedford, Ma.

MINGO, ANN - and Isaac Company

MINGO, CHARLES - and Lydia Jeffers

MINGO, MARY - and Charles Durfee

MIONEAMIE - and Tuspaquin

MITCHELL, EMMA - and Jacob Safford

MOHO, ABIGAIL - Punkapog Indian, and Ceasar Elisha

MOHOOIT, HANNAH - and Robert Autenet, Dartmouth, int. Nov. 10, 1740

MOIT, SARAH - of Dartmouth and Moses Sochonish int. June 27, 1782

MOMISCO - George of Hassanamisco Tribe and Christian woman

MOONEY, PRIMUS - of Stoughton, Ma. and Mary A.

MOSES, RUTH - and Cuffee Slocom, of Dartmouth, Ma., July 9, 1747

MOSES, TITUS - and Rebecca Opechus, Jan. 3, 1719, Scituate, Ma.

MUCKAMUG, PETER - Hassanamisco Tribe and Sarah Robbins

MUCKAMUG, SARAH - d. Indian Sarah, and Aaron, body servant to Col. Joe Whipple of Providence, R.I. ca. 1730, at home of Wm. and Mary Page

MUSQUNTDOWAS - and Meekenump

MYE, WILLIAM - of Mashpee and Roxanna Mann

NAANASHQUAW - and Naanishcow (John Thomas)

NANAMPASHAMET - and Squaw Sachem

NATTOOTUMAU - (HANNAH) and John Nahnosoo

NEPTUNE, FRANCES JOSEPH - m. Mary Chapman

NILES, ANDREW - s. James and Abigail (Johnson) Niles, and Fanny A. Fowler

NILES, LUCY - d. James and Barbara (Poquainup) Niles, and John Seketer; res., lots 32, 52, Brothertown, NY

NILES, MARY - d. James and Barbara (Poquainup) Niles, and Nathan Pendleton

NILES, PHEBE - d. James and Abigail (Johnson) Niles, and John Collins Fowler

99

MARRIAGES

NILES, PHEBE - d. James and Barbara (Poquainup) Niles, and Joseph Wauby; res., lot 33, Brothertown, NY

NILES, RHODA - d. James and Barbara (Poquainup) Niles, and Charles (1) and Daniel Wauby (2); res., lots 30, 31, Brotherown, NY

NILES, SOLOMON - s. James and Abigail (Johnson), and Cordelia Fowler, d. Lorenzo Fowler

NILES, JAMES - s. James and Jerusha Niles, and Barbara Poquiantup (Poquainup); res., lots 41, 42, Brothertown, NY

NILES, JAMES - grandson of James and Barbara (Poquainup) Niles and son of James, married Abigail Johnson; res., lot 93, Brothertown, NY

NILES, JOHN - s. James and Abigail (Johnson) Niles, and Harriet Fowler, d. David Fowler

NINIGRET, GEORGE - and Sarah

NINIGRET, THOMAS - and Molly Drummer and Mary Whitfield, 1761, Apr. 23, Newport, R.I.

NOKA, NANCY - d. Sam Noka and George Cheeves

NUMMOCH, SARAH and Moses Suchamus of Plymouth Nov. 28, 1751

NUMMUCH, HOSEA and James Frances of Plymouth Sept. 28, 1743

NUMMUCK, SILAS and Dinah Lamb, Dec. 27, 1750, Scituate, Ma.

NUNCKSEW, ELISABETH and Ichabod Prince of Dartmouth, Ma., Nov. 29, 1764

NUNCKSEW, JEMIMAH and Cuff Freeborn (Negro) of Dartmouth, Ma., May 26, 1768

NUNCKSEW, MARY - of Dartmouth, Ma. and Edward Allmy, May 26, 1768

OBADIAH (Obediah), ABIGAIL - and Prince Pond of Dartmouth, Ma., Apr. 30, 1774

OBADIAH (Obediah), JOHN - of Dartmouth, Ma. and Deborah Netewcash of Chilmark, Apr. 11, 1752

OBADIAH (Obediah), SARAH - of Dartmouth, Ma. and Thomas Cuff of Swanzey, Dec. 3, 1768

OCCUM, AARON - s. Samsom Occom, and Ann Robin, d. Samuel Robin, Wangunk Tribe, Middletown, Ct.

MARRIAGES

OCCUM, CHRISTIANA - d. Samson Occom, and Anthony Paul; res., Brothertown, NY, lot 10

OCCUM, JOSHUA - s. Joshua and Sarah Occum, and Eunice of Pequot Tribe

OCCUM, LUCY - d. Joshua and Sarah Occum, Mohegan Tribe, Mohegan, Ct., and John Tantaquidgeon

OCCUM, OLIVE - d. Samson, Solomon Adams; res., lot 52, Farmington, Ct., Tunxis Tribe

OCCUM, TABITHA - d. Samsom Occom, and Joseph Johnson, Dec. 2, 1773; res., Mohegan, Ct.

OHKOH, JOHN - and Sarah Hossueit, Dec. 9, 1757, Gay Head Congregational Church, Gay Head, Ma., Rev. Zachary Hossueit

PAGE(PEGIN), DEBORAH - of Dartmouth and Lonnon, Negro, June 14, 1782

PAGE(PEGIN), HOPE - of Freetown, and David Slocum of Dartmouth, Ma.

PALMER, JOSEPH - and Martha Waukeet; res., Wisconsin

PANCE, SAMUEL, Jr. - and Abigail Hossueit, Jan. 3, 1758, Gay Head, Ma., Rev. Z. Hossueit

PANUE, JOASH - and Rode Sauwamog, Jan. 11, 1769, Gay Head, Ma., Rev. Z. Hossueit

PANUPUHQUAH,DINAH - and Henry Ahhunnut (Jannohquisso)

PAPENEAU, SIMON - and Marcy Akoochik, Nov. 13, 1750, Gay Head, Ma., Rev. Z. Hossueit

PATIENCE, JANE - of Wareham and Wonyst Prince (Negro) Feb. 14, 1766

PAUL, ABIAH and Recol Degrass, int. Feb. 13, 1805

PAUL, BATHSHEBA - d. George and Lucy Paul, and George Scippio, s. Obadiah and Elizabeth (Fowler) Scippio; res., Wis.

PAUL, ELIZABETH - d. Samson and Hannah (Brushel), and Ezekiel Wiggins

PAUL, GEORGE - and Lucy; res., lot 23, Brothertown, NY

PAUL, JOHN - and Penelope; res., lot 4, Brothertown, NY

PAUL, MOSES - s. George and Lucy Paul, and Rachel Scippio, d. Obadiah and Elizabeth (Fowler) Scippio

MARRIAGES

PAUL, NATHAN - s. John and Penelope Paul, and Sarah
Skeesuck, d. Daniel Skeesuck; res., lot 136, Brothertown,
NY

PAUL, NELSON - s. Sampson and Hannah Brushel, and Lura
Fowler, d. B.G. Fowler; res., Brothertown, NY

PAUL, SAMPSON - s. Anthony and Christiana (Occom) Paul,
and Hannah Brushel, d. Samuel Brushell

PAUL, SILIS - & Martha Pomit, Nov. 8, 1764, Gay Head,
Ma., Rev. Z. Hossueit

PAUL, SOLOMON - and (2) Martha (Waukeet) Palmer; res.,
Manchester, Wis. and (1) Hannah Adams, d. Samuel Adams

PECHAUHER, SUSANNAH - and Simon Panu (Paunyoo)
Oct.14, 1802, Chilmark,Ma.

PEGAN, EDGAR EUGENE - of Peagan Tribe, and Emma
Buck of Columbia Pt., Ct.

PEGAN, GEORGE M. - s. James M. and Hannah (Vickers)
Pegan, and Candace Caperton

PEGAN, JAMES - s. Edgar Pegan, and Hannah Vickers, d.
Mary (Curless) and Christopher Vickers of Thompson, Ct.

PEGIN, DEBORAH - and Lonnon of Dartmouth, Ma.
June 14, 1782

PESHAUKER, JANE - d. Thomas Peshauker of lot 14,
Brothertown, NY, and Isaac Wauby; res., White River, Ind.

PESHAUKER, THOMAS - s. Thomas Peshauker, and
Abigail; res., lot 65, Brothertown, NY

PEQUIT, ALICE - and Paul Cuff, Feb. 14, 1783

PEQUIT, ISAAC - of Dartmouth and Deborah Ceasor
Nov. 4, 1765

PEQUIT, JAMES - of Dartmouth and Alice (Ailce) Abel
Oct. 18, 1772

PERRY, WILLIAM - Fall River Tribe, and Louisa of
Penobscot Tribe

PETERS, AURILLA - d. John and Elizabeth Peters, and
John Baldwin; res., lots 3, 106

PETERS, GEORGE - and Eunice Wampy, d. Elijah
Wampy; res., lots 118, 125, Brothertown, NY

PETERS, JERUSHA - d. George & Eunice (Wampy)
Peters and Josiah Charles

MARRIAGES

PETERS, OLIVER - s. Elizabeth Peters, and Anne; res., Brothertown, NY, lot 29

PETERS, JOHNSON - and Mary Cooper, 1807, Oct.

PETERS, SAMUEL - and Sally Jeffers, 1839, Oct. 4, and Frances A. Loring

PETERS, SOPHIA - and George J. Belain, 1835, Oct.16

PETERS, WILLIAM - s. John and Elizabeth Peters, and Bridget; res., lot 148, Brothertown, NY

PHARAOH, BENJAMIN - and Damaria Pharaoh; res., lot 124, Brothertown, NY

PHARAOH, EPHRAIM - and Phebe Fowler; res., lots 17, 132, Brothertown, NY

PHARAOH, TEMPERANCE - d. Ephraim and Phebe (Fowler) Pharaoh, and B. G. Fowler

PHILLIP, JEMIMAH - and Simon Joel, May 8, 1758, Gay Head, Ma., Rev. Z. Hossueit

PHILLIP, SILAS - and Jude Joel, Dec. 14, 1753, Gay Head, Ma., Rev. Z. Hossueit

PIERCE, CAROLINE - and Royal Torbit of Taunton, Ma. Nov. 20, 1820, Middleboro, Ma.

POCKNET, JACOB - and Reliance, Mashpee Indians

POLLOCK, NANCY - d. Mingo Pollock and Indian Woman of Dudley Tribe, m. Christopher Curliss

POQUIANTUP (POQUENUP,UPPUIQUIYABTUP) AARON - and Lovinia; res., lot 130, Brothertown, NY

POQUIANTUP, ESTHER - d. Samson and Esther Poquiantup of Pequot Tribe, and Jacob Fowler

POQUIOM, BEN - s. Major Ben Poquiom, grandson of Uncas, and Ann, d. of Ceasar, granddaughter of Oweneco; res., Mohegan territory, Ct.

POTTER, AMY - d. Samson Potter, and Jacob Fowler; res., lot 141, Brothertown, NY

POTTER, HANNAH - d. Daniel and Mary Potter, and William Dick; res., lot 135, Brothertown, NY

PRINCE, MARTIN - and Esther, of Indian descent:

PRINCE, MARY - d. of Mary Prince Weston, and Ceser Slocum, Dartmouth, Ma., Apr. 26, 1775

PRINCE, MARY - and Ceasor Russell, of Dartmouth, Ma., Jan. 2, 1788

MARRIAGES

PRINCE, SYLVESTER - of Marshfield, Ma., and Susanna Rider, Dec. 25, 1765

PRINTER - of Hassanamisco Tribe and Benjamin Speen

PRINTER, ABIGAIL - d. Amy Printer, Hassanamisco Tribe, and Andrew Abraham of Hassanamisco Tribe

PRINTER, MARY - of Hassanamisco Tribe and Zechariah Tom

PRINTER, PATIENCE - of Hassanamisco Tribe and Ceasar Lawrence

PRINTER, SARAH - Hassanamisco Tribe, and Peter Lawrence

QUAM, HANNAH - and Reuben Barber, Barkhamstead, Ct.

QUAM, MARY - and Gum Webster, Barkhamstead, Ct.

QUAM, MERCY - and Isaac Jacklin, Barkhamstead, Ct.

QUAM, POLLY - and William Wilson, Barkhamstead, Ct.

QUAM, SAMUEL - and Miss Green of Sharon, Ct.

QUAM, SOLOMON - and Miss Hayes, Barkhamstead, Ct.

QUANAMPOWITT, JAMES (JAMES WISER, MUMINQUASH) - and Mary Ponham

QUANAWIN, JOSEPH - of Dartmouth and Hannah Peckham int. Oct. 26, 1788

QUANNAWIN, JAMES - of Dartmouth and Polly Slocum int. Dec. 24, 1787

QUANNAWIN, PETER - of Tiverton and Martha Job of Dartmouth, Ma., May 23,1763

QUANSETT, THOMAS - and Naomi Menekish of Monomoy

QUACH, NANCY - (int. Quash) and Jeremiah Burk, Mustee Oct. 25, 1784

QUASON, AMOS - and Mercy Ned, 1738

QUASON, DAVID - and Sarah Cowet

QUASON, SARAH - and Stephen Maskuck (Wasnechsuk)

QUINNEY, CATHERINE - and Solomon Aumpaumut

QUINNEY, ELIZABETH - and Jacob Seth

QUINNEY, ELECTRA - and Daniel Adams, Mohawk and Cherokee Editor

QUINNEY, JOSEPH - and Cynthia Simons

QUINNEY, LYDIA - and Capt. Hendrick Aupaumut

RABILL, JAMES - and Esther Rabill, Mar. 2, 1764, Gay Head, Ma., Rev. Z. Hossueit

MARRIAGES

ROBBINS, DAVID - of Mashpee and Henretta Tobins

ROBBINS, DAVID - of Farmington, Ct., Tunxis/Wangunk Tribes and Hannah; res., lot 116, Brothertown, NY

ROBERTS, THOMAS - and Abigail; res., lot 102, Brothertown, NY

ROBINSON, ZERVIAH - and Cato White, May 28, 1812, Middleboro, Ma.

ROLLINS, HARRIET - and Oliver Gardner of Mashpee, Ma.

ROSELY, JOHN - and Jane Squin, Dec. 30, 1812, Middleboro, Ma.

ROSO, SILAS - and Phebe Squin Nov. 20, 1791, Middleboro, Ma.

SACHEMUS, SUSANNA - of Plymouth and Adam Allen (Negro) Nov. 2, 1761

SAMPSON, ABEL - s. James and Esther Simons, d. John Simons; res., lot 15, Brothertown, NY

SAMPSON, ALMIRA J. - d. Clara D. and Rozina Matthews, and O. D. Dick

SAMPSON, CLARK D. - and Rozina Matthews; res.,Wis.

SAMPSON, GEORGE - s. James, and Lucena Dick, d. William Dick; res., lot 112, Brothertown, NY

SAMPSON, JANE - d. George and Lucena (Dick) Sampson, and John Foss

SAMPSON, SOPHIA - d. George and Lucena (Dick) Sampson, and John R. Coyhis. s. John and Martha (Dick) Sampson

SASSAMON, ELIZABETH - and Jonathan Pusuckqunush March 30, 1757

SASSAMON, MARY - and Aaron Pusuckqunush, Sept. 17, 1756

SAUWAMOG, DEBORAH - and John Simon, Jr., Mar. 22, 1768, Gay Head, Ma., Rev. Z. Hossueit

SCIPIO, CELINDO - d. Obadiah and Elizabeth (Fowler) Scipio, and James Simons, s. Emanuel Simons; res., Kaukauna, Wis.

SCIPIO, DANIEL - of Dartmouth and Sarah Thomas Oct. 8, 1768

SCIPIO, GEORGE - and Bathsheba Paul

SCIPIO, RACHEL - and Moses Paul

MARRIAGES

SEKETER, CHARLES - s. John and Lucy (Niles) Seketer, and Abigail Wiott, d. Thomas Wiott

SEKETER, CHARLOTTA - d. John and Lucy (Niles) Seketer, and John Wilbur

SEKETER, GRACE - d. John and Lucy (Niles) Seketer, and Samuel Skeesuck; res., Brothertown, NY, lot 69

SEKETER, JOHN - s. John Seketer, and Lucy Niles, d. James Niles; res., lots, 32, 52 Brothertown, NY

SEPIT, MICAH - of Plymouth and Mary Sepit, 6, 25, 1756

SEPIT, PHEBE - and Amos Jeffrey, Nov. 10, 1763, Plimpton, Ma.

SESSETOM, ALICE - and Joseph Daggett

SETAM, ABILL - and Mary Hossueit, 29th day, Gay Head, Ma., Rev. Z. Hossueit

SHERMAN, GEORGE - and Mary A. Hamilton

SHERMAN, WILLIAM - and Nancy Hopkins, New London, Ct.

SHERMAN, SIANUM - and Ketcanomin (Josiah)

SIMMONS, ELIZABETH - and David Fowler

SIMMONS, SIMON - and Thankful Ward both of Freetown, Dec. 30, 1773, by Rev. Silas Brett

SIMON, ROBERT - and Sarah Thomas, Mar. 26, 1764, Middleboro, Ma.

SIMONS, ABRAHAM - s. Sarah, and Sarah Adams, d. John Adams; res., lot 12, Brothertown, NY

SIMONS, CYNTHIA - d. Emanuel Simons of lot 111, Brothertown, NY, and Joseph M. Quinney, Stockbridge Tribe

SIMONS, EMELINE - d. John Mason and Lucy Simons, and Jaques

SIMONS, ESTHER - d. John Mason and Lucy Simons, and Abel Sampson; res., 115, Brothertown, NY

SIMONS, JOHN MASON - s. Emanuel Simons, and Lucy; res., 107, 108, Brothertown, NY

SIMONS, SARAH - d. John Mason and Lucy Simons, and James Fowler; res., lots 102, 111, Brothertown, NY

SKEESUCK, AARON, s. John Skeesuck, and Lydia Brushel, d. Samuel Brushel

MARRIAGES

SKEESUCK, ABRAHAM - s. Samuel and Mary (Seketer) Skeesuck, and Adeline Dick, d. Paul Dick; res., lot 70, Brothertown, NY

SKEESUCK, CHARLOTTE - d. John and Anne Skeesuck, and William Johnson; res., Wis.

SKEESUCK, DANIEL - s. Samuel and Mary (Seketer) Skeesuck, and Sylvia Abner; res., lot 80, Brothertown, NY, 1832, Wis.

SKEESUCK, DAVID - s. John Skeesuch, and Eunice Charles, d. Josiah Charles; res., Wis.

SKEESUCK, FANNY - d. Samuel and Mary (Seketer), and Hezekiah Fowler

SKEESUCK, JOHN - s. John and Anne Skeesuck, and Hannah Galin; res., lots 22, 26, 83, Brothertown, NY

SKEESUCK, LUCY - d. Samuel and Mary (Seketer), and Henry Welch

SKEESUCK SAMUEL - s. Daniel and Mary Seketer; res., Wis.

SKEESUCK, SARAH ANN - d. John Skeesuck and Elkanah Dick

SKI...., JOSEPH - and Martha Gashim, Feb.15, 1760, Gay Head, Ma., Rev. Z. Hossueit

SLOCUM, DAVID - a Mustee, of Dartmouth, Ma. and Hope Page of Freetown, Nov. 1771

SLOCUM, POLLY - Mustee, of Dartmouth, Ma. and Abner Elisha, Nov. 1784

SLOCUM, POLLY - and James Quannawin of Dartmouth, int. Dec. 24, 1787

SMITH, THOMAS - and Wealthy Squin Mar. 2, 1832, Middleboro, Ma.

SOCLBASIN - Mrs. and Deacon Tikn Sokepsn

SOLOMON, MARY - of Dartmouth and Pero Cogshall, Oct. 4, 1767

SOUSOACO (JEPTHA) - and Eastor

SPEEN, BENJAMIN - and d. Moses Printer, Hassanamisco Tribe

SPEEN, MARY - of Natick, and Jonathan Peagan of New Roxbury, int. pub. May 31, 1730

MARRIAGES

SPRAGUE, LYDIA A. - of Dudley Tribe and Lemuel Henry

STEPHENS, STEPHEN - and Sarah Jethro

SUCHAMUS, MOSES - of Plymouth, Ma. and Sarah
Numoch, Nov. 28, 1751

SUCKONASH, PETER - of Dartmouth and Mallinda
Carpenter of Dartmouth, Ma., Nov. 13, 1816

SUCKONASH, SIMON - of Little Compton, R.I. and
Deborah Richmond of Dartmouth, Ma., June 9, 1786

TALLMAN, JOSEPH - and Elis Hohpen, Dec. 30, 1768,
Gay Head, Ma., Rev. Z. Hossueit

TALLMAN, MARCY - and Isaac (Silas) Johnson, Mar. 28,
1766, Gay Head, Ma., Rev. Z. Hossueit

TALLMAN, MARY - and John Joel, May 8, 1771,
Gay Head, Ma., Rev. Z. Hossueit

TALLMAN, SARAH - and Zacharay Hossueit, Jr., Dec.,
1760, Gay Head, Ma., Rev. Z. Hossueit

TANTAQUIDGEON, LUCY - d. Lucy (Occom)and John
Tantaquideon, and Peter Teecomwas

TAPUM, MARY - and John Commocho, of Natick, Ma.,
int. pub. Sept. 6, 1736

TAUCOMMONER, ESTHER (Easter) - and Tobey Smith,
Negro, July 10, 1773, Freetown, Ma.

TEECOMWAS, CYNTHIA - d. Lucy (Tantaquidgeon) and
Peter Teecomwas, and Hoscott

TEECOMWAS, SARAH - d. Lucy (Tantaquidgeon) and
Peter Teecomwas, and Jacob H. Fowler

TERRY, ABIGAIL JANE - d. Nero and Abby Cooper of
Freetown, Ma., Troy Indian, and James Tillman Lindsey,
Fall River, Ma., July 31, 1842

TERRY, EBENEZER - of Troy and Betsey Allen of
Dartmouth, Ma., April 22, 1813

TERRY, MARTHA - of Dartmouth, Ma., and James Solomon
Oct. 4, 1787

TERRY, MERCY - of Assonet, Ma. and Caleb Johnson of
Cannonville, Ma., July 31, 1806, New Bedford, Ma.

TERRY, NERO - and Abigail Cooper of Freetown, Ma.,
Feb. 16, 1791

TERRY, PHOEBE - of Freetown, Ma., and Joseph Daggett
of Sherborn, Ma., Aug. 6, 1752, by Rev. S. Brett

MARRIAGES

TERRY, STEPHEN - and Maria, Fall River Indians, res., Middleborough, Ma.:

THOMAS, JACOB - and Damaris Adams, d. Solomon Adams; res., lot 109, Brothertown, NY

THOMAS, JAMES - and Mary, Grafton Indian

THOMAS, LEAH - and Jacob Chalkcum of Natick, Ma., March 31, 1730, Oliver Peabody, Minister of the Gospel

THOMAS, SARAH - and Amos Francis of Natick, Ma., int. pub. Oct. 11, 1730

THOMAS, SOLOMON - and Sarah Abraham, of Natick, int. pub. Oct.11, 1730

THOMPSON, LYDIN - and Silas Kelly, Mashpee Indians

THOMPSON, SAMUEL and Lucy Canady, Dec. 2, 1820, Middleboro, Ma.

TOBEY, EPHRAIM - of Mashpee and d. Moses and Mercy Pocknett

TOCKQUENETT, ELISHA - and Margaret Johnson, Dec. 21, 1769, Chilmark

TOCQUENETT, ELIZABETH - and William Weeks, 1797, Chilmark

TOCQUENETT, PEGGY Jr. - and Joseph Gersham, Aug. 22, 1796, Chilmark

TOCQUENETT, SUSANNAH - and Thomas Cooper, Jr. , Dec. 13, 1798, Chilmark, Ma.

TOCUS, JOSEPH - of Charlestown, R.I., and Grace Crosley, d. George Crosley; res., lot 59, Brothertown, NY (1813-1834)

TOGOOSIN, MATTHEW - and Mary Akoochok, 1769, Gay Head, Ma., Rev. Z. Hossueit

TOHQUN, PASHONIS - and Joseph David, Nov. 1, 1754, Gay Head, Ma., Rev. Z. Hossueit

TOM ELIZABETH - and William Robinson, Natick, Ma., Sept.17, 1735, Oliver Peabody, Pastor

TOM, ZECHARIAH and Mary Printer, b. Feb. 1719, d. Moses Printer, m. ca. 1748, Hassanamisco Tribe

TORBIT, LEVI - and Rachel Harden Mar. 18, 1796, Middleboro, Ma.

TOUCEE, AARON - s. Benjamin and Elizabeth Curricomb, and Lydia Brushell

MARRIAGES

TOUCEE, BENJAMIN - s. David and Sarah Towsey of Tunxis Tribe, and Elizabeth Curricomb, d. Andrew Curricomb; res., Brothertown, NY, lot 20

TOUCEE, DAVID - s. Benjamin and Elizabeth Curricomb, and Eunice Charles, d. Josiah Charles; res., Wis.

TOUCEE, SARAH ANN - d. Benjamin and Elizabeth Curricomb,and Elkanah Dick; res., Brothertown, NY, lot 31

TOWANAH, JOSEPH of Dartmouth and Patience Prince of Dartmouth, Ma., Dec. 30, 1768

TOWOREY, PATIENCE and Abraham Lawton, a Mustee, of Dartmouth, Ma., Nov. 14, 1778

TOXCOIT, JAMES - a Narragansett, and Barsha; Brothertown, NY, lot 19

TUHIE, JEREMIAH - s. John and Sarah Tuhie, and Jerusha Charles, d. George (Tohoy) Peters; res., Brothertown, NY, lot 8

TUHIE (TOHOY), JOHN - a Narragansett, and Sarah; res., Brothertown, NY, Lots 11, 18

VANDERHOOP, JOHN PROSPERE - s. Wm. A.and Beulah Salsbury, and Abby A. Corsey, d. Landon and Julia F. (Jeffers) Corsey, m. 1871, Jan. 15

VANDERHOOP, WILLIAM ADRIAAN, - b. 1816, Parimaribo, Surinam and Beulah Salsbury, d. John Salsbury and Naomi Accouch, m. 1837, Mar.26

VANDERHOOP, WILLIAM A. Jr. - s. Wm. A and Beulah Salsbury, and Louisa T. Wood, m. 1871, Jan.15

VICKERS, CHRISTOPHER - s. Joseph Vickers, and Rhoda (Rhoby) Coffee

VICKERS, CHRISTOPHER - s. Christopher and Rhody (Coffee) Vickers, and Mary Curless of Burrillville, R.I.

WAUBY, CYNTHIA - d. Joseph and Phebe (Niles) Wauby, and Thomas Dick

WAUBY, ISAAC - s. Joseph and Phebe (Niles) Wauby, and Mary Jakeways; res., Wis.

WAUBY, ISAAC - s. Roger and Mary Wamby, and Jane Patchauker, d. Thomas Patchauker; res., lot 3, Brothertown, NY

WAUBY, JAMES - s. Joseph and Phebe (Niles) Wauby, and Eunice Dick, d. Paul Dick; res., Wis.

MARRIAGES

WAUBY, JOSEPH - s. Roger and Mary Wauby, and
Phebe Niles, d. James Niles; res., lot 33, Brothertown, NY

WAUBY, ROGER - and Mary; res., lot 3, Brothertown, NY

WAMPY, CLARINDA - d. Elijah and Elizabeth (Peters)
Wampy, and Jacob Scippio

WAMPY, ELIJAH - s. Elijah and widow Elizabeth Peters;
res., lot 15, Brothertown, NY

WAMPY, EUNICE - d. Eliajah Wampy, and George Peters

WAMPY, JERUSHA - d. Elijah Wampy, and Charles

WAMSLEY, HARRIET A. - of Gay Head, Ma. and Isaac
A. Rose, int. April 5, 1841

WAMSLEY, JANE - and John Rosier

WAMSLEY, PAUL - and Pheobe Jeffries

WAMSLEY, PHOEBE - and Silas Rosier

WAMSLEY, ZERVIA - and James Johnson, 1791, Dec. 4

WAPQUISH, PHILLIP - of Middleborough and Abiah
Hoswit, Nov. 4, 1746

WARWAME - and Miantonimo

WAUCUS, JAMES - s. James, grandson of early
Tunxis Chief, Wawawis, and Rachel; (Wowous,
Wawawis, Waukas, Wowowous) res., Farmington,
Ct., Stockbridge, Ma., Brothertown, NY

WAUCUS, JAMES - s. James and Rachel Waucus, and
Philena Adams, d. Solomon Adams and Olive Occum;
res., lot 9, Brothertown, NY

WAUCUS, PHILENA (ADAMS) - widow of James Waucus,
d. Solomon Adams and Olive Occum, and Thomas
Crosley; res., lots 76, 96, 97, Brothertown, NY

WAUKEET, JOSHUA - of Niantic Tribe, Niantic, Ct. and
Susannah; res., Brothertown, NY

WEEKS, TRISTRAM - and Mary Ann Cole, April 25,
1845, Gay Head, Ma.

WEEKS, TRISTRAM - and Margaret Francis, Gay Head

WEEKS, WILLIAM - and Elizabeth Tockquenett, Gay
Head, Ma., 1797

WENUCHUS - and Montowampate

**WENEPOYKIN (WINNERPURKEN, SAGAMORE GEORGE,
GEORGE NOHOSE)** - and Ahawayetsquaine

WHITTEN, HEPZIBAH - and Joel Assaquanhut

MARRIAGES

WICKCOM, DORCAS - and George Crank of Dartmouth, int. Jan. 6, 1773; m. Feb. 25, 1773, Dartmouth, Ma.

WIGGINS, CHARLOTTE - d. Samson Wiggins of lot 143, Brothertown, NY, and William Johnson

WIGGINS, EZEIKIEL - s. Martin and Louise (Hammar) Wiggins, and Elizabeth Paul, d. Samson Paul; res., Wis.

WIGGINS, JAMES - and Anne Curricomb, d. Andrew Curricomb; res., lots 122, 123, Brothertown, NY

WIGGINS, LEANDER - and Henrietta Brushell; res., Brothertown, NY

WIGGINS, MARTIN - s. Ezekiel and Elizabeth (Paul) Wiggins and Mary Ann Denny, of Oneida Tribe

WIGGINS, MARTIN - s. James Wiggins (Titus) and Anne Curricomb, d. Andrew Curricomb, and Louise Hammar; res., Brothertown, Wis.

WIOT, ABIGAIL - d. Thomas Wiot, and Charles Seketer; res., Brothertown, NY

WIOT, DANIEL - s. Thomas Wiot, and Rachel; res., Brothertown, NY, lot 88

WOMPANUMMOO, MARTHA - and Simon Coomes

WOMSQUON, JOSHUA - and Sarah Pettimee, int. pub. April 12, 1730, Natick, Ma.

WOSSONON, JEMIMA - and Aaron Gashim, Jan. 26, 1749/50, Gay Head, Rev. Hossueit

DEATHS

DEATHS

AARON, JOSEPH - s. Sarah Muckamug and Joseph Aaron, d. Aug. 1808, Grafton, Ma., Nipmunk/Hassanamisco Tribe

AARON, JOSEPH - body servant to Col. Joseph Whipple, d. 1768 Grafton, Ma., Nipunk/Hassanamisco Tribe

ABRAHAM, ANDREW - d. 1748; Hassanamisco Tribe

ABNER, RANDALL - d. 1852, Kansas; Pequot Tribe

AKOOCHUK - d. Nov. 14, 1714, Gayhead, Ma.

ADAM - d. ca. 1690, Chappaqquiddick, Ma.

ADAMS, ARTHUR - d. 1864, Sept. 2; Andersonville

ADAMS - SACHEM QUINNIPIAC TRIBE, - d. ca. 1800

ADAMS, SAMUEL - d. ca. 1800

ADAMS, SOLOMON - d. ca.1783

AHAWAYETSQUAINE (JOAN) - d. Poquanum of Nahant, Ma., d. 1685

AHHUNNUT, ABIGAIL - d. 1715, Sanchekantaket, Edgartown, Ma.

AHHUNNUT, DINAH - d. Panupuhquah of Monument, wife of Henry Ahhunnut (Jannohquisso) d. 1684, Nashowohkamuk

AHHUNNUT, HANNAH - wife (1) of John Momonequem, wife (2) of Job Ahhunnut, d. 1704, Chilmark, Ma.

AKOMPOWIN - brother of Chief Massasoit, d. 1676, June 22

AKOOCHUK - d. 1714, Nov. 14, Gayhead, Ma.

ALANOHCHANNUM, - wife of John Tackanash, d. 1720, at Nunpaug, Edgartown, Ma.

AMANHUT, JOHN - s. Wannamanhut, d. 1672, Mar; Martha's Vineyard, Ma.

AMMAPOO (ABIGAIL) - d. Cheshchaamog, d. 1710, Sanchecantacket in Edgartown, Ma.

AMOS - d. 1690, Chappaquiddick, Ma.

AMOS, ABIGAIL, d. Rachel and Jonathan Amos, d. 1711, Chilmark, Ma.

AMOS, ELISHA (ELISHA IANOXETT) - s. Amos Ianxoo, Sr., d. 1763, Takame (Tisbury)

AMOS, RACHEL - d. Miohqsoo, d. 1711, Chilmark, Ma.

ANNAMPANU (MAATTI) - granddaughter of Noatoasaet, Island sachem, niece of Mittark, d. 1715, Dartmouth, Ma.

DEATHS

ANTHONY, ELSE - d. ca.1790, Middleboro, Ma.

ANTHONY, JEREMIAH - d. Jan. 14, 1762, Middleboro, Ma.

ASKOMOPOO, ABIGAIL - d. 1710, Sanchecantacket

ASSANNOOSHQUE, (Old SARAH) - wife of James Cowkeeper, d. 1703, Edgartown, Ma.

ASSAQUANHUT (John Showkow) - d. 1690, Christiantown, Ma.

ASSAQUANHUT, HEPZIBAH - d. John and Jerusha Whitten, wife of Jowel Assaquanhut, d. Oct. 20, 1723, Tisbury, Ma.

ASSEWETOUGH - d. John Sassamon, granddaughter of Pessicus, d. 1696

ATTAMONCHASSUCK - Potonumecot Tribe; d. 1720

ATTOMON, ESTHER - d. 1762

ATTOMON, JOHN - grandson of Attamonchassuck, d. Jan. 23, 1744-45

ATTOMON, RICHARD - d. 1745, Jan.23

BRAND, JOANNA - d. 1851, Middleboro, Ma.

BRUSHELL, HENRY - d. 1864, Sept. 24, Wisconsin

BRUSHELL, LEMUEL - d. ca. 1827, Brothertown, NY

BRUSHELL, NANCY (Welch) - d. 1864, April 7, Wisconsin

BRUSHELL, SAM - d. 1882, Mohegan, Ct.

BUCHANAN, MARY (Johnson) - d. Patience (Durfee) and Thomas Buchanan, granddaughter of Mary (Mingo) and Charles Durfee, d. 1919

CANONICUS - NARRAGANSET GRAND SACHEM; d. 1667, July 2

CEASAR - Sachem of Mohegan Tribe; s. Oweneco, grandson of Uncas, d. 1723, Ct.

CHAPMAN, HERBERT - s. Mary Johnson Buchanan Chapman, descendant of Isaac Company, d. 1884

CHARLES, HANNAH - d. Rachel and Jonathan Amos, d. 1711, Tisbury, Ma.

CHARLES, JOSIAH - d. ca. 1828, Brothertown, NY

CHEESCHAMOG, CALEB - s. Homes Hole Sachem, Cheesechamut (Nickanoose), d. 1666, Ma.

CHUMMACK, LAURA - d. Sept. 7, 1839, Middleboro, Ma.

COCHEGAN, SOLOMON - d. 1794, Brothertown, NY

COMMUCK, THOMAS - d. Nov. 25, 1855, Brothertown, Wis.

DEATHS

COMMUCK, WORTHINTON - s. Thomas and Hannah (Abner) Commuck, d. Feb.1, 1863

CONONCHET (NENUNTENO) - d. 1676

COOMES, MARTHA - d. 1722, Nashouohkamuk (Chilmark, Ma.)

COOMES, SAMUEL - s. Hiacoomes, d. 1703, Nashouohkamuk (Chilmark, Ma.)

COOMES, SARAH - d. March 10, 1723, Chilmark, Ma.

COSHOMON, JOHANNA - wife of Samuel Coshomon, d. 1711, Sanchekantacket

COSHOMON, MARY - d. Jonathan Amos, wife of Eliah Coshomon, d. 1721-2, Chilmark, Ma.

COSHOMON, MARY - wife of Samuel Coshomon, d. 1691, Chilmark, Ma.

COYHIIS, WILLIAM - s. Ephraim Coyhis, d. May, 1804, Brothertown, NY

CROSLEY - d. 1866

DESHON, FELIX - d. ca. 1816, Brothertown, NY

DICK, ALEXANDER - s. Paul and Hannah (Fowler) Dick d. 1852, Kansas

DICK, ASA - s. Nathan and Eunice (Johnson) Dick, d. March, 1864, Cairo

DICK, ASA - s. Isaac and Cynthia (Brown) Dick, d. Sept. 13, 1843, Dickville, NY

DICK, FRANKLIN M. - s. Nathan and Eunice (Johnson) Dick, d. July 22, 1864, Vicksburg

DICK, ISAAC - s. Isaac and Cynthia (Brown) Dick, d. April 10, 1854, Wis.

DICK, LATON - s. William and Hannah (Potter) Dick, July 31, 1880, Brothertown, Wis.

DICK, MAHALIA - d. July 16, 1842, Middleboro, Ma.

DICK, ORLANDO - s. Nathan and Eunice (Johnson) Dick, d. Aug. 9, 1881

DICK, THOMAS - d. 1834, Wis.

DICK, THOMAS - s. Thomas and Deborah Dick, d. 1832, Wis.

DICK, WILLIAM - d. ca. 1814, Brothertown, NY

115

DEATHS

DICK, WILLIAM - s. William and Hannah (Potter) Dick, d. Sept. 7, 1866, Brothertown, Wis.

FOWLER, BENJAMIN GARRET - s. David and Hannah (Garret) Fowler, d. Dec.12, 1848, Wis.

FOWLER, DAVID - s. James Fowler, d. Mar.31, 1807, Brothertown, NY

FOWLER, DAVID - s. James Fowler, d. Feb.10, 1890, Brothertown, Wis.

FOWLER, JAMES - s. David and Hannah (Garret) Fowler, d. ca. 1830, Brothertown, NY

FOWLER, LUCIUS SYRENIUS - s. Jacob and Amy (Potter) Fowler, d. Feb. 23, 1886, Brothertown, Wis.

FOWLER, ORRIN GRIDLEY - s. Rhodolphus and Elizabeth (Dick) Fowler. d. May 13, 1862, Ship Is., Miss.

FOWLER, OSAMUS - s. Rhodolphus and Elizabeth (Dick) Fowler, d. Aug. 4, 1874, Brothertown, Wis.

FOWLER, SIMEON ADAMS - s. James and Patience (Dick) Fowler, d. Nov. 20, 1880, Brothertown, Wis.

FOWLER, WILLIAM - s. James and Patience (Dick) Fowler, d. Oct. 8, 1862, Perryville, Wis.

FRANCES, JOHN - s. Frances Joseph Neptune, Passamaquoddy Chief; d. 1875, Me.

FRANCES, SELMORE - s. Frances Joseph Neptune, Passamaquoddy Chief; d. 1881, Me.

FRANCIS, FRANK - d. Jan. 29, 1852, Middleboro, Ma.

FREEBORN, ESTHER - Grafton Indian Woman, d. 1808, Grafton, Ma.

GARRISON, MARY ELIZABETH - d. Alfred and Helen E. (Thomas) Garrison, d. April 6, 1928, New Bedford, Ma.

GOULD, KEZIAH HILL - d. Betsey (Gould) and James Hill, wife of Camoralsman Gould, d. 1844, Sept.15

GOULD, MALINDA - d. Phoebe Wamsley and Brister Gould, d. June 16, 1824, Ma.

HAMMER, HANNAH - d. Brothertown, N.Y.

HAMMER, HENRY - s. Samuel and Polly (Johnson) Hammer, d. Oct.15, 1862, Chaplin Hills

HAMMER, IRA - s. John Hammar, d. 1872, Wis.

HAMMER, JOHN - s. John Hammar, d. ca. 1823, Brothertown, NY

DEATHS

HANNIT, JAPHETH - s. Pamchannit , d. 1712, July 29, Martha's Vineyard, Ma.

HANNIT, JEDIDAH - s. Japheth and Sarah Hannit, d. 1725, Oct, 14, Chilmark, Ma.

HANNIT, JEREMIAH - s. Japheth Hannit, d. 1686, Chilmark, Ma.

HANNIT, SARAH - d. Kestumin, wife of Japheth Hannit, d. 1716-17, Mar.

HALL, RUBY GOULD - d. Phoebe Wamsley and Brister Gould, wife of Benjamin Hall, d. 1851

HARRY, PRUDE - d. Sampson and Eunice Pouquenup, buried in Deansville Cemetery, (Eunice) Brothertown, NY

HART, SIMEON - s. Nancy (Brushell) Hart, July 1, 1847, Wis.

HEMENWAY, FRANCIS - d. Oct. 10, 1842, Middleboro, Ma.

HEMENWAY, HEPSIBAH (CROSS) - wife of Jeffrey Hemenway, d. 1847, Worcester, Ma.

HILL, BETSEY GOULD - d. Phoebe Wamsley, granddaughter of Lydia Tuspaquin Wamsley, wife of James Hill, d. 1824, June 16, Ma.

HOPEWELL, SARAH - d. ca. April, 1704, Wethesfield, Ct.

HOWWANNAN, JOHN - d. 1678, Christiantown, Ma.

HUTTON, SAMUEL - d. ca. 1810, Brothertown, NY

IANXOO (IANXOQUISSOO, HENRY OHHUNNUT) - s. Ompahinit, d. 1724

JAMES, SAMUEL - s. James Cowkeeper and Old Sarah, d. 1715, Sanchekantacket in Edgartown, Ma.

JANAWANNIT - d. 1686, Nashouohkmuk (Chilmark, Ma.)

JANNOHQUISSOO - d. Feb. 1722-23, Nashan (Slocum's Island)

JANNOHQUISSOO (HENRY OHHUNNUT) - d. Dec.17, 1724, Christiantown, Ma.

JEHU - d. ca. 1690, Chappaquiddick, Ma.

JOHNSON, DAVID - s. Emanuel and Martha (Fowler) Johnson, d. 1896, Wis.

JOHNSON, EMANUEL - s. John Johnson, d. ca. 1834, Wis.

JOHNSON, EMANUEL P. - s. John W. Johnson, d. Oct. 27, 1857

117

DEATHS

JOHNSON, GAZELLE M. - s. John W. Johnson, d. April 20, 1846

JOHNSON, HENRY - s. John, d. Nov. 6, 1862, Perryville,Wis.

JOHNSON, JEREMIAH E. - s. John W. Johnson, d. Nov. 28, 1851

JOHNSON, JOHN - s. John Johnson, d. May 10, 1860, Wis.

JOHNSON, JOHN W. - s. John Johnson, d. Feb. 27, 1881, Brothertown, NY

JOHNSON, ORRIN G. - s. William and Charlotte (Skeesuck) Johnson, d. 1880

JOHNSON, ORVANDO F. - s. Emanuel and Martha (Fowler) Johnson, d. Aug.4, 1864, Wis.

JOHNSON, ROWLAND - Emanuel andMartha (Fowler) Johnson, d. 1897, Wis.

JOHNSON, WAYLAND L. - s. John W. and Rebecca (Abner) Johnson, d. April 4, 1870

JOHNSON, WILLIAM HENRY - s. Mercy (Terry) and Caleb Johnson

JOHNS, ALITHEA - d. Sept. 14, 1805, Grafton Indian woman, Grafton, Ma.

JOQUIBB, ELIZABETH MAMOHET - d. Mamohet, d. 1756, July 5, Ct.

JOSIAH, CHARLES - spouse of Jerusha Peters, d. ca. 1828, Brothertown, NY, lot 102

JULIAO, LYDIA (Gould) - d. Phoebe Wamsley, granddaughter of Lydia (Tuspaquin) Wamsley, d. 1855, June 22

KENUMP, ABIGAIL - d. Amos and Abigail Kennump, d. 1710, Chilmark, Ma.

KESOEHTAUT, ABIGAIL - d. Pahahahkuh and wife Munuhkishque of Chilmark, d. 1709, Chilmark, Ma.

KINDNESS, JAMES - s. Thomas and Phebe Kindness, d. Nov. 30, 1861, Brothertown, NY

KOHTOHKOMUT, SAMUEL - d. ca. 1690, Chappaquiddick, Ma.

KOKESAP, (LAZARUS) - d. 1677, Nunpang, Edgartown, Ma.

LABAN, PANU - s. Joash and Naomi Panu, d. Nov. 6, 1715, Gay Head, Ma.

DEATHS

LANNON, CHARLES - d. Oct. 9, 1841, Middleboro, Ma.

LAY, REBECCAH - wife of William Lay, d. 1708,
Martha's Vineyard, Ma.

LINDSAY, ABIGAIL JANE - d. Nero and Abby (Cooper)
Terry, spouse of James Tillman Lindsey, d. Aug. 17, 1860,
Fall River, Ma.

MAMOHET, ELIZABETH - d. 1756, July 5

MANHUT, ABIGAIL - d. Johan Ammanhut, d. 1685,
Nahouohkamuk

MANHUT, MARY - d. Hosia Manhut and wife Quakshmoh,
d. 1724, Apr. 8, Christiantown

MANHUT, MARY - wife of John Ammanhut, d. 1689,
Nashouohkamuk

MASHQUATTUHKOOIT (PAUL) - d. ca. 1688, Holmes Hole,
Martha's Vineyard, Ma.

MATTHEWS, (NAHNEHSHECHAT) - d. ca. 1690,
Chappaquiddick, Ma.

MATTHEWS, ELIPHALET (ADAMS) - adopted by Sarah
Adams Simons, d. Sept. 5, 1851, Wis. (Esquire, Matthews)

MATTHEWS, JOHN - s. Eliphalet and Elizabeth (Crosley)
Matthews, d. Feb. 24, 1883, Wis.

MATTHEWS, RANSOM - s. Eliphalet and Elizabeth
(Crosley) Matthews, d. June 13, 1866, Brothertown,Wis.

MIANTONOMO - s. Mascus, d. 1643

MISCO, DEBORAH - d. May, 1760; Hassanamisco
Indian Woman

MITCHELL, DELORES (CHIC-CHICCHEWEE)- d. Zerviah
(Gould) and Thomas C. Mitchell, granddaughter of Phoebe
Wamsley and Brister Gould, d. June 2, 1875, Ma.

MITCHELL, JANE W. - d. Zerviah (Gould) and Thomas C.
Mitchell, granddaughter of Phoebe (Wamsley) and Brister
Gould, d. March 28, 1840, Ma.

MITCHELL, JOHN - s. Zerviah (Gould) and Thomas C.
Mitchell, d. 1870, Sept. at sea

MITCHELL, THOMAS C. - spouse of Zerviah Gould, d.
1859, June 16

MITTARK, SACHEM of GAYHEAD - d. 1683, Jan. 20

MOMATCHEGIN, JOSHUA - d. 1703, Chappaquiddick, Ma.

DEATHS

MOMCHQUANNUM - wife of Sissetome, d. 1715, Sanchekantacket, Edgartown, Ma.

MOORE, CHARLES - d. July 6, 1841, Middleboro, Ma.

MOORE, CHARLES - d. July 20, 1842, Middleboro, Ma.

NAHNEHSHEHCHAT (MATTHEW) - brother of Kestumin, d. ca. 1690, Chappaquiddick, Ma.

NAHNOSOO, JOSEPH - s. John Nahnosoo, d. 1685, Nashouohkamuk (Chilmark, Ma.)

NAHPUNNCHTAU - wife of John Papamek, wife of Paatoohk, d. 1703, Christiantown, Ma.

NANAPASHAMET - GRAND SACHEM of MASSACHUSETT TRIBE; d. 1619

NASHCOMPAIT, JAMES - d. 1713, Pashkehtanesit (Tucker's Island)

NASHOKAU, STEPHEN - s. Nashohkow, d. 1713, Christiantown, Ma.

NEPTUNE, FRANCES JOSEPH - PASSAMAQUODDY GOVERNOR, d. 1844, Pleasant Pt., Me.

NEPTUNE, JEAN BAPTISTE (BAHGULWET) - s. Peter Paul Neptune, Chief of Passamaquoddy Tribe, d. Jan.6, 1778, Machias

NEPTUNE, MARY JOSEPH - d. Apr. 5, 1834, Pleasant Pt., Me.

NETAWASH, SIMON - d. 1693, Chilmark, Ma.

NICKANOOSE - NANTUCKET SACHEM, d. 1683

NILES, DREW - s. James and Abigail (Johnson) Niles, d. Sept.18, 1864, Wis.

NILES, JAMES - s. James Niles, d. Sept. 7, 1863, Wis.

NILES, SAMUEL - s. James and Abigail (Johnson) Niles, d. 1853, Wis.

NINIGRET, THOMAS - s. George, grandson of Chief Ninigret and wife Magnus, d. 1769

NOHNSOO, HANNAH - d. Cheshchaamug of Holmes' Hole, d. 1716, Tisbury (Nattootunmau)

NOQUITTOMPANY - d. 1690, Christiantown, Ma.

OCCUM, JOSHUA - s. Joshua and Eunice Occum, d. ca. 1782

OCCUM, EUNICE - s. Joshua and Eunice, d. April 1787

DEATHS

OHHUMUH, ELEAZAR - s. Caleb and Deborah Ohhumuh, d. 1698, Gayhead, Ma.

OHHUMUH, HENRY (JANNOHQUISSOO) - d. 1724, Christiantown, Ma.

OHQUANHUT, JERUSHA - d. Peter and Dorcas Ohquanhut, d. Nov. 4, 1714, Martha's Vineyard, Ma.

OHQUANHUT, LYDIA - d. Peter and Dorcas Ohquanhut, d. 1715, Martha's Vineyard, Ma.

OMPAN, JERUSHA - d. Josiah and Ruth Patumpan, d. 1721, Sept. 18; Tisbury, Ma.

OMPANY (KOMPANET, OMPPANE), ISSAC - s. Noquitompany, d. March 1716, Christiantown, Ma.

OMPANY, NAOMY - d. Isaac Ompany, granddaughter of Noquitompany, wife of Thomas Sasamon, d. May 21, 1726, Christiantown, Ma.

OMPANY, RACHEL - d. Isaac Ompany, wife of Daniel Wompanummoo, d. June 15, 1724, Christiantown, Ma.

ONEPENNY, SARAH - d. ca. May 1713, South Meadows, Hartford, Ct.

ONEPENNY, SARAH - d. ca. May 27, 1727, Hartford, Ct.

OONQUN, THOMAS - d. ca.1690, Chappaquiddick, Ma.

OSOOIT, MARGARET (MEEKSISHQUNE)- d. Tisbury Sachem, Keteanomin (Josiah) and wife Sianum, d. Dec. 5, 1723, Gayhead, Ma.

OWENECO - s. Uncas and the Daughter of Sassacus, d. 1715, possibly Montville, Ct.

PAAONIT, ABIAH - d. Jonathan and Rachel Amos, d. 1712, Chilmark, Ma.

PAAONIT, ELISHA - s. Paaonut, d. 1714, Martha's Vineyard, Ma.

PAGE, BARTON - s. Mahala (Durfee) Page, grandson of Mary Mingo and Charles Durfee, d. 1888

PAGE, CHARLES - s. Mahala (Durfee) Page, grandson of Mary Mingo and Charles Durfee, d. 1916

PAGE, MAHALA - d. Mary (Mingo) Durfee, grandson of Isaac Ompany and Ann Mingo, d. 1893

PALMER, JOSEPH - d. July 3, 1836, Wis.

PAMCHANNIT - CHILMARK SACHEM, d. 1672, Nashouohkamuk

DEATHS

PANNUNNUT (WILLIAM LAY) - d. 1690, Nashouohkamuk (Chilmark, Ma.)

PANU, JOASH - s. Annampanu, d. 1720, Aug., Martha's Vineyard, Ma.

PANUPUHQUAH - d. 1724

PASHQUNNAHHAMUN, SAMUEL - d. 1721, Tisbury, Ma.

PATTOMPAN - brother of John, Micah, Stephen, Daniel Shohkau, d. 1688, Tisbury, Ma.

PATTOMPAN, ELIZABETH - d. Josiah and Ruth Pattompan, d. July 6, 1710, Tisbury, Ma.

PATTOMPAN, PAUL (OLD PAUL) - d. 1676, Christiantown, Ma.

PATTOMPAN, RUTH - wife of Josiah Pattompan, d. 1722, Tisbury, Ma.

PAUL, DAVID - d. 1718, Nunpaug, Edgartown, Ma.

PAUL, MARY PALMER - widow of Joseph Palmer, wife of Solomon Paul, d. Jan. 26, 1874, Manchester, Wis.

PEAG, JOSEPH - s. Jacob and Sarah Peag, d. July 20, 1723, Christiantown, Ma.

PEAG, SARAH - d. Samson Cahkuhquit and wife Elizabeth, d. 1723, Oct. 30, Christiantown, Ma.

PEGAN, EDGAR - d. 1868

PEGAN, EDGAR EUGENE - d. Oct. 15, 1880, Thompson, Ct.

PEGAN, JAMES M. - s. Edgar Pegan, d. Aug. 25, 1892, Thompson, Ct.

PEGNECK, ELIZABETH - d. 1600, Oct. 20

PEHTAUATTOOH - brother of Pamchannit, d. ca. 1680, Martha's Vineyard, Ma.

PEOSIN, JOB - d. 1723, Sanchekantacket

PETERS, GEORGE - d. Rome, NY, Feb. 24, 1800

PETERS, WILLIAM - s. Oliver and Anne Peters, d. June 29, 1864, Dallas, Ga.

PHARAOH, EPHRAIM - d. ca. 1825, Brothertown, NY

POMIT, JANE - d. Jesse and Jane Pomit, 1716, Nashouohkamuk (Chilmark, Ma.)

POMPI - d. 1740, May 1

POMPMAHCHOHOO, JOSEPH - s. Pamanominnit, d. 1687, at Watshat, Martha's Vineyard, Ma.

DEATHS

POQUENUP, AARON - Nehantic Tribe, d. Dec. 2, 1835, Brothertown, NY

POQUENUP, ESTHER - Mohegan Tribe, d. Jan. 22, 1822, Brothertown, NY

POQUENUP, LOVINIA - wife of Aaron Poquenup, d. Aug. 14, 1835, Brothertown, NY

POQUIOM, BEN - s. Major Ben Poquiom, d. 1769, Ct.

POQUIOM, BEN (Major) - s. Uncas, grandson of Meekenump, d. 1725, Ct.

POQUIOM, ISAIAH - s. Ann and Ben Poquiom, grandson of Ceasar, Sachem of Mohegan Tribe, d. 1770

POQUIOM, POMPI - s. Ann and Ben Poquiom, grandson of Ceasar, Sachem of Mohegan Tribe; d. 1740

POTTER, SAMPSON - s. Daniel and Mary Potter, d. 1832, Brothertown, NY

POTTER, TOBIT - d. 1722, Christiantown, Ma.

PRINTER, SARAH - d. 1763, Grafton, Ma.

QUAM, ELIZABETH - d. 1820, Barkhamstead, Ct.

QUAM, MOLLY - d. 1820, Barkhamstead, Ct.

QUANAPOWITT (James Wiser, Muminquash) - s. Yawatta and Massachusetts Grand Sachem, Nanapashamet, d. 1712

QUANSETT, (MENEKISH) - d. 1730, Oct.; Chatham

QUANSETT, THOMAS - s. Quequaganet of Herring Pond, d. 1715, Monomoy

QUANNOOHUH, JESSE - s. Jeremiah and Hannah Quannoohuh, d. 1724, June 5, Christiantown, Ma.

QUATEATASHSHIT - Manomet Sachem, d. 1684

ROBBINS, HANNAH - d. 1827, Brothertown, NY

ROBBINS, RHODA - d. Hannah and David Robin, d. ca. 1814, Brothertown, NY

ROBINSON, AMY - d. Dec. 9, 1842, Middleboro, Ma.

SAMPSON, ABEL - spouse of Esther Simons, d. 1830, Brothertown,NY

SAMPSON, CLARK D. - spouse of Rozina Matthews, d. March 6, 1865, Wis.

SAMPSON, GEORGE - s. James Sampson, d. 1839, Brothertown, NY

DEATHS

SASSAMON, JOHN - d. 1674
SASSAMON, NAOMY - wife of Thomas Sosamon, d.
Isaac Ompany, d. May 21, 1726
SCIPPIO, OBADIAH - d. 1806, Brothertown, NY
SEIKNOUT, JACOB - s. Joshua Seiknout, d. 1734,
Chappaquiddick, Ma.
SEIKNOUT, JOSHUA - s. Seiknouet, Chappaquidick
Sachem, d. 1717, Chappaquiddick, Ma.
SEIMORE, SAPPIEL - grandson of Chief Frances
Joseph Neptune, Passamaquoddy Chief, s. Elective
Governor, Selmore Frances, d. 1903, ae. 93
SEKITCHAHKOMUN, ABIGAIL - d. 1722, Slocums
Island (Nashaun)
SEPET, JOHN - s. Kussepit, d. 1725, Manomet
SEPINNU, JAMES - brother of John Tackanash, d. 1683,
(Okokame) Christiantown, Ma.
SESSETUM, DEBORAH - d. 1724, Feb.12, Sanchekantaket
SESSETUM, REBECCAH - d. 1719, Sanchekantacket
SETUM, THOMAS - s. Sissetome, a Sanchekantacket
Sachem,d. 1694 (Thomas Sissetom)
SHOHKAU, STEPHEN - d. 1713
SHOHKAU, MICAH - d. 1690, Christiantown, Ma.
SIMONS, BEN - d. May 1831, Middleboro, Ma.
SIMONS, EMANUEL - d. 1806, Brothertown, NY
SIMONS, JAMES - s. James and Celinda (Scippio) Simons,
d. Jan. 25, 1898, Kaukauna, Wis.
SIMONS, JOHN MASON - s. Emanuel Simons, d. 1822,
Brothertown, NY
SIMS, JOEL - s. Pockqsimme, d. 1680, Christiantown,
Ma., Sanchekantacket
SKEESUCK, ARNOLD - d. ca. 1820, Brothertown, NY
SKEESUCK, ARNOLD - s. Arnold and B. G. (Fowler)
Skeesuck, d. March 1, 1877, Wis.
SKUHWHANNAN, JAPHETH - s. Nicodemus
Skuhwhannan and Bethia Hannit, d. 1715, Chilmark, Ma.
SHOHKAN, MICAH - d. 1690, Christiantown, Ma.
SHOHKAU, STEPHEN - Nashohkow, d. 1713, Tisbury, Ma.
SIOKUNUMAU - wife of Mechim, d. 1690, Martha's
Vineyard, Ma.

DEATHS

SISSETOM, BETHIE - d. Oggin (Haukim) and wife Hannah, d. October, 1721, Sanchekantacket

SISSETOM, DEBORAH - d. Caleb Sissetom, d. Feb.12, 1724, Sanchekantacket

SOCKAKONNIT, THOMAS - d. 1703, Edgartown, Ma.

SOCKAKONNIT, JACOB - s. Thomas Sockakonnit, d. 1721, Nunpaug in Edgartown, Ma.

SOGKOHKONNOO, THOMAS - d. 1703, Sanchekantacket

SOMANNAN, JOB - s. Somannan of Takame (Tisbury), d. 1718, Christiantown, Ma.

SOOPASUN, HANNAH - d. Joel and Sarah Soopasun, d. 1723, May 12, Christiantown, Ma.

SPANIARD, JAMES - d. 1721, Chilmark

SPEEN, HANNAH - d. 1718, Natick, Ma.

SQUAMAMIE, MOLLY (BARBER) - wife of James Squamamie (Chaughm), d. 1820, Barkhamstead, Ct.

SQUIN, BEN - s. Lydia, d. April 22, 1799, Middleboro, Ma.

SQUIN, JEAN - d. Lydia, d. April 13, 1794, Middleboro, Ma.

SMITH, THOMAS - d. March 7, 1872, ae. 62, Middleboro, Ma.

SMITH, WILLIAM - d. Feb. 17, 1875, ae. 61, Middleboro, Ma.

TACKAMASUN, STEPHEN (STEPHEN COMMASNIM, COMMASUNNUN, TOGOMASUN) - s. Wuttattakkomasun, d. 1708, Chilmark, Ma.

TAKNASH - Martha's Vineyard Minister, d. 1684

TAWANQUATUCK, SATCHEM - d. ca. 1670, Martha's Vineyard, Ma.

THOMAS, ALICE - d. March 19, 1766, Middleboro, Ma.

THOMAS, SAMUEL - d. March 6, 1759, Middleboro, Ma.

THOMAS, SARAH - d. July 3, 1785, Middleboro, Ma.

THOMAS, JOHN, Sr. (NAAMISHCOW) - d. 1727, Natick, Ma.

THOMAS, MARY - wife of James Thomas, a Grafton Indian Woman, d. Aug. 20, 1797

TILER, HANNAH - d. Mequane and wife Susannah, d. 1723, Sanchecantacket in Edgartown, Ma.

TOCKANASH, JOHN - d. 1683-4, Jan. 22, Martha's Vineyard, Ma.

TOUWANQUATACK - d. ca. 1670, Martha's Vineyard, Ma.

DEATHS

TUHIE, JOHN - d. Dec. 14, 1811, Brothertown, NY

TUPHAUS - d. 1704

TUPHAUS, BETHIA - d. Bethia and William Tuphaus, d. 1704

TUPHAUS, JOB - s. William and Bethia Tuphaus, d. 1714

TUPHAUS, WILLIAM - s. William and Bethia (Amos) Taphus, d. 1703, Chilmark, Ma.

TOBIT (Tobit Potter) - s. Elizabeth Uhquat, d. 1722, Okahame, (Christiantown, Ma.)

TARRAMUGGAS - s. Sowheag, Chief of Wongunks of Middletown, Ct., d. before 1705

UHQUAT, ELIZABETH - d. 1723, Christiantown, Ma.

UNCAS - s. Oweneco and wife Meekenump, d. 1682; Ct.

UNCAS, ANN - d. of first Ben Uncas, Sachem of Mohegan Tribe; d. July 31, 1741

UNCAS, SAMUEL - grandson of Uncas, great grandson of Sassacus, d. July 31, 1741, Ct.

VICKERS, CHRISTOPHER - s. Joseph Vickers, Dec. 6, 1862, Thompson, Ct.

VICKERS, CHRISTOPHER - s. Christopher Vickers

VICKERS, MARY (CURLESS) - d. Christopher and Anne (Pollock) Curless of Narragansett Tribe, d. Jan. 27, 1897, Oxford, Ma.

WAMPAMOG (Mr. Sam) - d. ca. Oct., 1689, Martha's Vineyard, Ma.

WAMSLEY, BENJAMIN - s. Phoebe (Jeffries) and Paul Wamsley, d. 1790, June 22

WAMSLEY, JANE - d. Phoebe (Jeffries) and Paul Wamsley, d. 1794, June 15

WAMSLEY, PHOEBE - d. Lydia Tuspaquin and Wamsley, granddaughter of Mercy Felix and Benjamin Tuspaquin, d. 1839, Aug. 16, Ma.

WANAHTAK, ISAAC - of Christiantown, d. 1715, Falmouth, Ma.

WASHAMON - d. ca. 1690, Chappaquiddick, Ma.

WAUWOMPUHQUE, ABEL - s. Abel Wauwompuhque, d. Oct. 1, 1722, Martha's Vineyard, Ma.

WAUWOMPUHQUE, ABEL - brother of Sachem Mittark, d. 1713, Nashwohkamuk

DEATHS

WENEPOYKIN - (Sagamore George), s. Nanepashemet and Squaw Sachem, d. 1684, Lynn,Ma.

WESCHIPPAU, JEREMIAH - s. Elisha Wesachippau, d. 1705, Chilmark, Ma.

WILLIAMS, JANE GOULD - d. Phoebe Wamsley and Brister Gould, wife of John Williams, d. 1844, May 27

WOMPANUMMOO, RACHEL - d. Isaac Ompany and wife Elizabeth, d. June 15, 1724, Christiantown, Ma.

WONOHAWUAHAM (SAGAMORE JOHN) - s. Nanepashemet and Squaw Sachem, d. 1633, Dec. 5; Lynn, Ma.

WUNNANAUHKOMAUN - d. 1676, Christiantown, Ma.

WUTTAHHANNOMPISIN (DAVID)- d. 1688, Gayhead, Ma.

WUTTINOMONOMIN - of Gayhead, Ma., d. 1698

WUTTUNUNOHKOMKOOH - wife of Pamchannit, d. 1675, Martha's Vineyard, Ma.

WUUUTTONTAEHTUNNOOH, KATHERINE - d. Mechim and wife Suioknuman, d. 1718, Sanchecantacket in Edgartown, Ma.

YONOHHUMUH - d. 1698, Gay Head, Ma.

SOURCES

ADAMS, DWIGHT R., GEORGE CARMICHAEL AND GEORGE B.
CARPENTER. 1880. Narragansett Tribe of Indians, Report To The
House Of Representatives. Providence: E.L. Freeman & Co.

ARNOLD, JAMES. 1889. Narragansett Historical Register, Volume
I. Narragansett Historical Publishing Company

ATWATER, FRANCIS. 1897. History of Kent, Connecticut.
Meriden, Connecticut: The Journal Publishing Co

BARRY, WILLIAM. 1847. History of Framingham, Massachusetts,
Including the Plantation, From 1640 to The Present Time.
Boston: James Munroe And Company.

BEALS, CHARLES EDWARD. Passaconaway In The White
Mountains. Boston: Richard G. Badger. The Copp Clark Co.,
Limited.

BONFANTI, LEO. 1968. Biographies and Legends of the New
England Indians. Wakefield, Massachusetts: Pride Publishing,
Inc.

BURGESS, EDWARD S. (1926) 1970. The Old South Road Of
Gayhead. Reprint. Dukes County Intelligencer.

CHIPMAN, R. MANNING. 1860. The History of Harwinton,
Connecticut. Hartford: Press Of Williams, Wiley and Turner,
Park Printing Office.

COREY, DELORRAINE PENDRE. 1898. History of Malden. Cam
bridge, Massachusetts: Univ. Press

DEFOREST, JOHN W. 1853. History of the Indians of Connecticut
From The Earliest Known Period to 1850. Hartford, Connecti
cut: Wm. Jas. Hamersley.

SOURCES

DENISON, FREDERICK. 1878. Westerly and Its Witnesses. Providence, Rhode Island: J. A. and R. A. Reid. Drake, S.F. 1861. Biography and History of the Indians of North America, Boston.

EARLE, JOHN MILTON. 1861. Indians of Massachusetts. Senate-No. 96.

EARLE, JOHN MILTON. 1862. Report To The Governor and Council Concerning The Indians of the Commonwealth. Massachusetts House Document No. 215.

FREEMAN, FREDERICK. 1858. The History Of Cape Cod: The Annals of Barnstable County And Of Its Several Towns, Including The District Of Mashpee. Boston: Geor. C. Rand & Avery.

HALL, BENJAMIN H. 1858. History of Eastern Vermont. New York: D. Appleton & Co.

HEBARD, LEARNED, THOMAS KINGSBURY AND HENRY HAVEN. 1861. Report Of The Commissioners on Distribution of Land of The Mohegan Indians. Hartford, Connecticut: Printed by Order of the Legislature.

HUDSON, ALFRED SERENAO. 1889. The History Of Sudury, Massachusetts, 1638-1889. Sudbury: The Town of Sudbury.

JACOBUS, DONALD LINES. 1974. Families Of Ancient New Haven, Vol. VII. Baltimore: Genealogical Publishing Co., Inc.

LEWIS, ALONZO AND JAMES R. HEWHALL. 1865. History of Lynn, Including Lynnfield, Saugus, Swampscot and Nahant. Boston: John L. Shorey, Publisher.

SOURCES

LOVE, W. DELOSS. 1899. Samson Occom and the Christian Indians of New England. Boston and Chicago: Pilgrim Press.

MANWARING, CHARLES WM. 1906. A Digest Of The Early Connecticut Probate Records. Hartford, Connecticut: R. S. Peck & Co., Printers.

MAYHEW, EXPERIENCE. 1727. Indian Converts: Or, Some Account Of The Lives and Dying Speeches of a consider able Number of the Christianized Indians of Martha's Vineyard, in New England: London: Samuel Gerrish.

MILLER, WM. DAVIS, ESQ. 1936. Ancient Paths To Pequot. Providence, Rhode Island: E. L. Freeman and Norman M. Isham Company.

MUNNELL, MICHAEL. 1993. American Indian Marriage Record Directory for Ashland County, Wisconsin, 1874-1907. Diluth, Minnesota: Chippewa Heritage Publications.

NILES, GRACE GREYLOCK. 1912. The Hoosac Valley Its Legends and Its History. N.Y. and London: P. Putnam's Sons.

ORCUTT, SAMUEL. 1882. Indians of the Housatonic and Nau gatuck Valleys. Hartford, Connecticut: Univ. Press.

PIERCE, EBENEZER W. 1878. Indian History, Biography and Genealogy: Pertaining to the Good Sachem Massasoit of the Wampanoag Tribe, and his descendants. North Abing ton, Massachusetts: C. G. Mitchell.

SHATTUCK, LEMUEL. 1835. History of the Town of Concord; Middlesex County, Massachusetts From Its Earliest Set tlement to 1832. Boston. Russell, Odiorne and Company.

SOURCES

SHELDON, GEORGE. 1895. History of Deerfield, Massachusetts, Volume 1, Deerfield: Pocumtuck Valley Memorial Association.

SMITH, WILLIAM. 1909. History of Chatham, Massachusetts Formerly the Constablewick or Village of Monomoit. Hyannis, Massachusetts. F. B. and F. P. Goss, Publishers.

STILES, EZRA. 1916. Extracts From The Itineraries And Other Miscellanies of Ezra Stiles, D. D. LLD 1755-1794.

TRUMBULL, BENJAMIN. 1808. A Complete History of Connecticut, Vol. I. New London: H. D. Utley.

WATSON, W. L. 1949. History of Jamestown. John F. Green Co., Inc.

WHITE, WILLIAM. 1856. Report of the Commissioners To Determine Title of Certain Lands Claimed by Indians at Deep Bottom, In The Town of Tisbury, On The Island of Martha's Vineyard. Boston: William White, Printer To The State.

WORTH, HENRY BERNARD. 1896. Quakerism on Nantucket Since 1800. Nantucket: Nantucket Historical Association.

www.ingramcontent.com/pod-product-compliance
Lightning Source LLC
Chambersburg PA
CBHW070809290326
41931CB00011BB/2179